Literary Criticism and Cultural Theory

Edited by
William E. Cain
Professor of English
Wellesley College

A Routledge Series

Literary Criticism and Cultural Theory

William E. Cain, *General Editor*

AESTHETIC HYSTERIA

The Great Neurosis in Victorian
Melodrama and Contemporary Fiction

Ankhi Mukherjee

Routledge
New York & London

Routledge
Taylor & Francis Group
270 Madison Avenue
New York, NY 10016

Routledge
Taylor & Francis Group
2 Park Square
Milton Park, Abingdon
Oxon OX14 4RN

© 2007 by Taylor & Francis Group, LLC
Routledge is an imprint of Taylor & Francis Group, an Informa business

Printed in the United States of America on acid-free paper
10 9 8 7 6 5 4 3 2 1

International Standard Book Number-13: 978-0-415-98140-8 (Hardcover)

Library of Congress Cataloging-in-Publication Data

Mukherjee, Ankhi.
   Aesthetic hysteria : the great neurosis in Victorian melodrama and contemporary fiction / by Ankhi Mukherjee.
      p. cm. -- (Literary criticism and cultural theory)
   Includes bibliographical references and index.
   ISBN-13: 978-0-415-98140-8 (acid-free paper)
   ISBN-10: 0-415-98140-9 (acid-free paper)
   1. English drama--19th century--History and criticism. 2. Melodrama, English--History and criticism. 3. English fiction--20th century--History and criticism. 4. Hysteria in literature. 5. Neuroses in literature. 6. Identity (Psychology) in literature. 7. Psychoanalysis in literature. I. Title.

PR728.M4M85 2007
822'.052709--dc22
                                                 2007008381

Visit the Taylor & Francis Web site at
http://www.taylorandfrancis.com

and the Routledge Web site at
http://www.routledge.com

For Saumya Banerjee

Contents

Preface

Since Plato identified hysteria as a disease caused by the uterus, a voracious "animal inside an animal," it has had very bad press: "suffocatio," "suffocation of the uterus," or, interchangeably, "suffocation of the mother," "chorea lascivia," "Maid's, Nun's and Widow's Melancholy," "the wandering womb," "mysteria," even "genital causes," "*grand fallace*," "fraud." Even after Freudian psychoanalysis changed the somaticist orientation of hysteria studies into a mentalist one, and three decades after Hélène Cixous identified with the hysterical patient as "the Absolute Woman," "hysterical" remains a misogynist epithet of opprobrium, ridicule, and abjection. At best, hysteria is understood as recuperating the materiality of the body from its deconstruction in language. At worst, it is an exhibitionist psychopathology, an over-the-top mode of excess and overflow that threatens reason, civilization, and consciousness. The proposed study on hysteria looks less at the "mad" corporeal body of hysteria than the body of language which surfaces in its lesions and breakdowns, and argues for a constitutive relationship between literature and hysteria. While writers from Shakespeare to Poe to Kafka to Woolf have preempted the symptomatology and metaphorics of hysteria for their sheer histrionic potential, this project looks transversally through hysteria-as-literary-effect at a more insidious hysteria of the signifier in certain kinds of imaginative writing. When literature poses the question of hysteria, it seems to exceed authorial intention or agency to testify to unspeakable intensities outside language and consciousness. The hysterical symptom or diagnostic in literature becomes, in the words of Ellie Ragland, "a place of knowledge . . . that knows nothing of itself."[1] This study examines a range of hysterical symptoms in literature, which are not readily interpretable symbols or metaphors of hysteria, but persist instead as gaps, feints, blind spots, and resistances within the text.

In 1994, hysteria was excluded as a syndrome from the fourth edition of the official register of mental diseases, the *Diagnostic and Statistical Manual of Mental Disorders:* for literary critics fascinated with hysteria, this was an exit as impactive as Ibsen's Nora's conclusive door-slamming on the Western cultural imaginary.[2] With this excision, hysteria lost its ontic register as it were to become a gleam in the eye of a curious assortment of academics: literary scholars, narratologists, feminists, psychoanalysts, social historians and historians of medicine, philosophers, anthropologists, and art historians. The historian Mark Micale notes "a burst of professional interest in the *history* of the disorder" in the past twenty-five years, "the very period that has witnessed the decline of hysteria as a medical diagnosis."[3] *The International Classification of Diseases* and DSM testify to the gradual disappearance of the polysymptomatic forms of the disease, as recorded by Jean-Martin Charcot and Sigmund Freud. Hysteria has been reconceptualized, in these directories, as the "factitious illness disorder," "histrionic personality type," "psychogenic pain disorder," and given other irreverent appellations. "Where has all the hysteria gone?" the psychologist Roberta Satow dramatically asked in 1979. My own intervention in hysteria studies follows the lead provided by medical historians and scholars in the humanities who reclaimed hysteria after psychiatrists hastily pronounced it dead in the twentieth-century.

In the late 70s, feminist theorists such as Hélène Cixous, Catherine Clément, and Christina von Braun saw in hysteria a model of disenchanted feminine subjectivity in a patriarchal culture. More recent feminist interventions describe what Kahane terms "the psychopoetics of hysteria" (xiv) and its implication in Victorian and modernist narrative discourse. Monique David-Ménard's *Hysteria from Freud to Lacan: Body and Language in Psychoanalysis* (1989), and *Hysteria Beyond Freud,* edited by Sander Gilman et al (1993), are key texts in what Mark Micale calls the "New Hysteria Studies," which trace the epistemological history of hysteria against the ideological contexts in which that history was written. Other influential work on hysteria in the 1990s focused on the extraordinary mimetic quality of hysteria, and its postmodern forms. According to Elaine Showalter, the "New Hysterics" constitute an eclectic and international group: alien abductees, victims of satanic ritual abuse, sufferers of the Gulf War Syndrome, the "incest camp" (which claims childhood sexual abuse on the basis of memory recovered in hypnosis), and the inheritors of racial and cultural traumas. Unlike Freud's "case studies," however, contemporary hysterical patients are reluctant to trace their disorders to psychological causes, and blame external sources instead: unknown viruses, sexual molestation, chemical warfare, satanic conspiracy, and alien infiltration. And this is where the "New Hysterians" step in to speak for hysteria, and make readable the scrambled codes of its own brand of social communication.

As Elaine Showalter points out in her 1997 monograph on hysteria, during the past decade, the "hysterical narrative" has become one of the most popular formulations in literary criticism. Showalter's own *The Female Malady: Women, Madness, and English Culture, 1830–1980* (1991) and *Hystories: Hysterical Epidemics and Modern Media* (1997), George Rousseau's monograph-length " 'A Strange Pathology': Hysteria in the Early Modern World, 1500–1800" (1993), Katherine Cummings's *Telling Tales: The Hysteric's Seduction in Fiction and Theory* (1991), Mark Micale's *Approaching Hysteria: Disease and Its Interpretations* (1995), Peter Logan's *Nerves and Narratives: A Cultural History of Hysteria in 19ᵗʰ-Century British Prose* (1997), Elin Diamond's *Unmaking Mimesis: Essays on Feminism and Theater* (1997), and Elizabeth Bronfen's *The Knotted Subject: Hysteria and its Discontents* (1998) have successfully emerged from the crossroads of psychoanalytic theory, feminist literary criticism, and the history of medicine. Diana Fuss's *Identification Papers* (1995) briefly examines the cultural production of (mass) hysteria, and Juliet Mitchell's *Mad Men and Medusas: Reclaiming Hysteria* (2000) describes the universality and pervasiveness of hysteria. Finally, Rachel P. Maines's entertaining and edifying *The Technology of Orgasm: "Hysteria," the Vibrator, and Women's Sexual Satisfaction* (1999), is a pioneering technological history of the vibrator as a medical tool for the treatment of hysteria.

Micale's intriguingly titled *Approaching Hysteria*—will the quest hero "get" hysteria before it gets him?—is arguably the most encyclopedic book on hysteria in recent years. Micale, a relentless historiographer of hysteria, promotes hysteria studies for bringing about a happy collaboration between imaginative literature and psychological medicine. The bridge category of hysteria, he argues, is increasingly useful in understanding psychic disorders in an advanced psychiatric age. In his account of literary representations of hysteria, the interaction between psychoanalysis and literary criticism is mediated through "the talking body." While Micale records the history of interconnections between fiction and diagnostic theory, he does not, however, elaborate on the aesthetic register of literary appropriations of hysteria. His approach is representative of other cultural reappraisals of hysteria in recent years in that while he upholds the centrality of the nervous body in modern writing culture, and illustrates the productive exchange between cultural representations and medical codifications of hysteria, he privileges the implicit purposiveness or truth-content of hysterical performance over its expressiveness. My project addresses this lack in hysteria studies by focusing on the hysteric as a recurrent character type in English literature from the nineteenth-century to the present, on the intertextuality of the medical and cultural scripts that influence literary scenarios organized around hysteria, and the very nature of an aesthetic experience of hysteria. Literary examples include both postmodern thematizations of hysteria and more automatic, or less knowing, acts of hysteria in literature. I focus on three significant modes of hysterical acting-out: emotional overload and the speaking body (in Victorian melodrama), repetition compulsion (in Charles Dickens's autobiographical fiction and the postmodern phenomenon of canon revision), and traumatogenic verbal nonfluency (representations of stuttering and other anomalies in the flow of speech in war literature). The literary texts chosen for this exercise are sensationalistic and extravagant, albeit each in its singular way, and the heuristic I put in place to read such textual performances can also be termed sensational in that it provides a constitutive dimension for the theater of pleasure and pain, sickness and health, or repression and expression in hysterical narratives.

To add to the previous scholarship on literature and hysteria, I want to focus my analysis as specifically as possible on the hysteric model of desire, which is forever "wanting," and the hysteric mode of articulation, which presents without representing, or performs without symbolizing, converting a repressed thought or fantasy not to ideation, but to a corporeal condition. In the words of Juliet Mitchell, "beneath the flamboyant pantomime of the hysteric's seductive behaviour is the experience of a body that is not there."[4] The problem of this absent body—as I discuss in detail in Chapter 1—explains the ontological uncertainty of hysteria. For the hysteric, the body has gone missing, due to improper sexualization or trauma, mental and/or physical. The hysteric however, does not acknowledge the loss, and circumscribe it with words. Loss or lack often leads to a compensatory representation, but the hysteric's *lack* of loss makes the body feel materially nonexistent—because un-symbolized—but experientially existent, and excessive to a fault, returning to the site of its disappearance to exact its symbolic due. In hysteria the mind-body dualism collapses, for the hysteric experiences passions in the mind as well as the body. Conversion, as Freud understood it, implies this mysterious leap from mind to body, where a remark, which is felt to be like a slap in the face, actually results in a neuralgic twitch. So, in hysteria we have a substantial, embodied mind, and an abstracted body, which acts like the mind. Words are thing-like, pure idea is equivalent to pure sensation, and saying is doing, not a representation of doing.

The first chapter is the theoretical introduction to the themes of my book. In this chapter I work through definitions of hysteria and touch on the medical-historical background from Freud to Lacan against which hysteria has been conceptualized and categorized. I focus in particular on Freud's understanding of hysteria as predicated on disgust. Freud's, and later, Lacan's, definition of disgust is linked to their mapping of desire. Desire and disgust, in their foundational psychoanalytic work, are both messily related to an enjoyment in which the desire for incorporating the object (of desire) cancels itself in an aversion for incorporation. To use Kantian terms, disgust is a state of unslakable yearning, and like pure taste, it eschews actual tasting. Hysterical *jouissance* is a drive toward fusion that seeks to negate itself—it comes to nothing, destructuring itself over and over in intransitive repetition. Finally, I draw parallels between Adorno's conceptualization of the aesthetic sphere and Lacan's theorization of hysteria, and argue for a radical expressionism which is not easily homogenized and assimilated in the socio-symbolic.

The next chapter, "Too Much, Too Little: The Emotional Capital of Victorian Melodrama," looks at nineteenth-century illegitimate theatre. Victorian melodrama teems with subjectivities trapped in the discontinuity between the imaginary and the real, mad women and sometimes men suffering from unfixable desires or living out traumas. Melodrama is particularly visual: in the "acting out" of the hysteric—both verbal, as in syntactic displacements, and physical, as expressed by gestural language—one is provoked to read ideographs, locate signifying elements, and recuperate speech. However, instead of assuming an analytical position vis-à-vis the hysteric, and attempting to render the lack or gaps in her consciousness construable, this chapter addresses and evokes the alienation and scission in the field of language, the continual failure of self-representation, the failed self-identity of hysterical subjectivity.

In this chapter I also explore the possibility that melodramatic excess gives the slip to key tenets of psychoanalysis like oedipality, the splitting function of language, and the politics of sexual difference. Victorian melodrama gives us hystericized modernity: it has a metaphoric relationship to what Henry James characterized as a feminine, nervous, hysterical, chattering, canting age. I begin my discussion with Douglas Jerrold's play for "minor" theatres, *Black-Ey'd Susan* (1829), and trace the arc of melodramatic expressionism through domestic melodramas like *Masks and Faces* (1852), *Lady Audley's Secret* (1863), and the psychological "thriller" *Bells* (1871), to the theatrical realism of Pinero's *The Second Mrs Tanqueray* (1893). Melodrama's "more"—its characteristic overload of affect and hysterical inability to limit or close plot structures, its privileging of the plural over the universal, and subversion of the law—gives definition to a new cross-gender or confused-gender erotic and aesthetic.

In the third chapter, "'Missed Encounters': Repetition, Rewriting, and Contemporary Return to Charles Dickens's Great Expectations," I link questions of narrative function theoretically to those of repetition and return in hysteria. I look at Dickens's repetitious and hysterical writing in *Great Expectations* (1861), with its constant returns to the past, the returns of the past in the form of repressed material, and the vanishing point of the system of life-writing where it fails to integrate itself. Repetition here is not recollection, but a series of failed and missed encounters with history (and a past that inheres in the present). For Dickens, to write is to give over to the compulsion to repeat—that which is refused or repudiated in the formation of his bourgeois authorial subjectivity continues to determine it negatively. There is poetic justice indeed in postmodern reworkings of Dickens's great novel of returns and rewriting. In this chapter I look at extrapolations of the classic in Kathy Acker's *Great Expectations* (1982) and Sue Roe's *Estella* (1982) before reading Peter Carey's brilliant pastiche, *Jack Maggs* (1997), with Freud's and Lacan's differing notions of hysterical repetition.

The last chapter of the book, "Broken English: Neurosis and Narration in Pat Barker's *Regeneration* Trilogy," examines male hysteria and the link between hysteria and trauma through war narratives. This chapter revisits questions of repetition and the death drive brought up in Chapter 3 through a study of the anxiety neurosis of stuttering. Lacan relates trauma to one's identity, and relation to another, and an ethical responsibility to what he calls the "real," a palpable order of effects, which persists in language and being although it lacks an imaginary-symbolic language consciousness. Trauma is non-referential in the sense that it is not fully perceived as it occurs: in this formulation, one encounters trauma by belatedly enduring *and* surviving it in a series of recuperative departures. Pat Barker's *Regeneration* trilogy (1991–1995) is one such departure, opening up a luminous space of knowing in the moment of movement from trauma to recovery. Barker fictionalizes the renowned Cambridge psychologist Dr. W. H. R. Rivers as a chiasmic figure who, while in charge of curing war neurosis, also suffers a non-passive endurance of the Great War. With references to famous stutterers in Virginia Woolf's *Mrs Dalloway* (1925), Herman Melville's *Billy Budd* (1924), and James Joyce's *Finnegans Wake* (1939), I develop, in the course of my argument, an analytics of stuttering. The stutter is the performative in language, a speech act, a rupture in speech through which the body suppurates non-referential signs. In the context of war neuroses, I read that rupture at once as a private traumatic symptom and a mode of conveying a sense of shattered public or national identifications.

In an interview with Jean-Luc Nancy titled "Eating Well" (*Who Comes After the Subject?*), Derrida compares the dominant schema of subjectivity to symbolic anthropophagy: in a world of exchange one devours the other and lets oneself be devoured by him. He characterizes Western subjectivist metaphysics as eating, speaking, and thereby interiorizing the all-other. It is my argument in this book that hysteria studies has continued relevance in the humanities if only because the ontology of the hysteric remains one of the starkest reminders of a decentered and divided subject, and a negatively determined metaphysics. Hysteria expresses desire in terms of disgust, a turning away, turning its back on the homely wisdom of eating well. The hysteric "mouth" does not represent the logocentric expressive system, but that which it cannot include: the vomitive.

A theorization of disgust provides a valuable hermeneutic tool to imagine the end(s) of hermeneutics, and the inadequacy of theory. The "disgusting" is that which is non-readable, non-idealizable, unintelligible, and inassimilable: it stands for heterogeneous elements that give the lie to full and present meaning. Disgust is the name for an obscene intimacy with the object as well as a strenuously maintained distance from it. It is a sensuous moment-in-vanishing, the prototype of an aesthetic experience that finally surmounts its bodily character, of a desire that is intellectual and emotional. The shudder is a good starting place for theory, theory understood as a heuristic and not a fallacy that mistakes its own image for concretion, as Adorno cautions in *Negative Dialectics*. My readings of literary case studies of hysteria, whether expressed in the expropriativeness of emotion in melodrama, the anxiety of repetition in Dickens, or an eroticized death drive in trauma, all testify to a primal estrangement between subject and sign which subsequently becomes the terms of a transitive engagement.

Theory is a "desiring dialectic best exemplified by the discourse of the Hysteric," claims Jean-Michel Rabaté in his extended meditation on the subject in *The Future of Theory*.[5] Like hysteria, theory is an iterable discourse that commits a catachresis of identity and knowledge. In the conclusion to my book, I urge the necessity to rethink and remake hysteria studies, linking it to the "impossible" profession and possibility of theory.

NOTES TO THE PREFACE

1. Ellie Ragland, *Essays on the Pleasures of Death: From Freud to Lacan* (New York: Routledge, 1995), 123.
2. The DSM, published by the American Psychiatric Association, is the main diagnostic reference of mental health professionals in the USA.
3. Mark Micale, *Approaching Hysteria: Disease and Its Interpretations* (Princeton: Princeton UP, 1995), 4–5. According to Micale, "the final quarter of the twentieth century, it appears, is experiencing an efflorescence of

historical interest in hysteria to match the great medical preoccupation with the disease a century ago." Micale notes that there have been roughly four hundred publications on the topic, all of them historical in nature, in the last ten years.

4. Juliet Mitchell, *Mad Men and Medusas: Reclaiming Hysteria* (New York: Basic Books, 2000), 34.

5. Jean-Michel Rabaté, *The Future of Theory* (London: Blackwell, 2002), 15.

Acknowledgments

I am grateful to Liz Thompson and Max Novick at Routledge for picking my book for publication and to William Cain for accepting it in the Routledge Literary Criticism and Cultural Studies series.

Aesthetic Hysteria began as a dissertation in the English Department at Rutgers, The State University of New Jersey. I am immensely grateful to my mentor and preceptor, Derek Attridge, for his guidance and encouragement. Thank you for feeding the theory habit while making me aware of untheorizable particulars and for forcing me to practice a lucid prose style.

Thank you to my PhD director, Carolyn Williams, who opened many doors for me, particularly to the garden path that led to Theory School at Cornell. If this project has an originary moment, it must be when I first read Victorian theatre with you. I would like to thank you for defining my melodramatic imagination.

I am grateful to a cracking dissertation committee: Derek Attridge, Elin Diamond, Maud Ellmann, and Carolyn Williams. I could not have hoped for better dialogues or more formidable interlocutors. I thank you for your wit, open-mindedness, your arch and bemused commentary on the margins of papers, and finally for the overwhelming affirmation that followed the completion of each task.

A long line of great teachers has shaped this work. I cannot catalogue all the gifts, or adequately give thanks, but remain endlessly grateful to Isobel Armstrong, Rosemarie Bodenheimer, Elaine Chang, Steve Connor, Diana Fuss, Marcia Ian, Frances Restuccia, Bruce Robbins, and Elaine Showalter.

To my dear friends from graduate school, Anthony Alessandrini, Somnath Baidya Roy, Carol Dell'Amico, Matthew Kaiser, Vanessa Manhire, Nicole Nolan, thank you!

The PhD thesis became a book as I taught and researched at the University of Oxford. Robert Young facilitated a crucial break in Oxford when I was elected to a lectureship in 2002, and has been the very best kind of intellectual influence and ally since. I cannot thank him enough. I am indebted to wonderful colleagues and friends at Oxford: Josephine McDonagh for tireless professional and other advice, and Stephen Heyworth, Eri Hotta, and Bernard O'Donoghue for making my first years at Wadham fruitful and happy.

I am grateful to my parents, Chitra and Chandrachur Mukherjee, and sisters, Nayan and Dithi, for their constant love in an inconstant world. My loving thanks to Tiyash who has put up with her bookish mother's work habits and moods with a nonchalance bordering on understanding. Finally, the dubious honour of being the dedicatee for a monograph on hysteria goes to the most unhysterical character I know: my husband Saumya Banerjee. I give my first book to the person who has most enabled, motivated, worried about and wished for it.

Two of the chapters appeared in article form in journals and are reprinted with the kind permission of the publishers:

An early version of Chapter 4 appeared as "Stammering to Story: Neurosis and Narration in Pat Barker's *Regeneration*" *Critique: Studies in Contemporary Fiction* 43:1 (Fall 2001): 49–63. Reprinted with permission of the Helen Dwight Reid Educational Foundation. Published by Heldref Publications, 1319 18th Street, NW, Washington, DC 200036–1802. www.heldref. org. Copyright © 2001.

A version of Chapter 3, "Missed Encounters: Repetition, Rewriting, and Contemporary Returns to Charles Dickens's *Great Expectations*," appeared in *Contemporary Literature* 46:1 (Spring 2005): 108–133. Reprinted with permission of the University of Wisconsin Press, 1930 Monroe Street, 3rd floor, Madison WI 53711–2059. Copyright © 2005.

Chapter One

Introduction: "Stuck in the Gullet of the Signifier": Desire, Disgust, and the Aesthetics of Hysteria

In their critique of Kafka in *Kafka: Toward a Minor Literature,* Gilles Deleuze and Felix Guattari mention the emancipatory potential of writing "like a dog (but a dog can't write—exactly, exactly)" (26). Mystifying and absurd as this suggestion is, it yields, on further reflection, a very savvy theorization of formless expressivity, or the practice of opposing "a purely intensive usage of language to all symbolic or even significant or simply signifying usages of it" (19). Deleuze and Guattari here are discussing the possibilities of "minor literature," a singular and minor usage of a major language. Minor literature does not necessarily rise from a minor language, and is rather that which a minority (though not necessarily an ethnic one) constructs within a major language.

> he who has the misfortune of being born in the country of a great literature must write in its language, just as a Czech Jew writes in German, or an Ouzbekian writes in Russian. Writing like a dog digging a hole, a rat digging its burrow. And to do that, finding his own point of underdevelopment, his own *patois,* his own third world, his own desert. (18)

Writing like a dog, for Deleuze and Guattari, is similar to writing like a foreigner, sans entitlement or identity papers. When they enjoin us to write like an animal, the emphasis is not on *like,* but on *animal,* on metamorphosis, not metaphor or acting like something. It is a model of writing without subjectivity or agency, and of traversing zones of indetermination that lead to new synapses and new connections. The writer is not a master but an animal *and* a writing machine, aiming for perfectly unformed and materially intense expression, signs that do not designate. Like Kafka he makes a minor use of a major language (Prague German). Like Artaud he wrenches cries and gasps from French. Like Woolf she wallows in a rich destitution, coaxing a schizophrenic mélange out of an arid language. The writer of minor literature is a foreigner, forced to live in a language not his own. Or she feels like an outsider in her own language, like a nomad or immigrant, inhabiting the margin without a sense of belonging in its crammed space.

Minor literature, thus, is an unlimited becoming, a "deterritorialization" (16) which invents creative lines of escape for language. It dismantles subjectivity and disorganizes syntax to make it coincide simultaneously with "the barking of a dog, the cough of the ape, and the bustling of a beetle" (26). It brings language "slowly and progressively to the desert" (26), to its inherent underdevelopment, and attunes it to the polylingualism of repressed voices. This book looks at texts that practice the politics of what Deleuze and Guattari identify as minor literature, through representations of hysteria. Hysteria can be seen as both the consummation and ruin of the signifier. It signifies spectacularly through the symptom, yet cannot be interpreted away in the manner of other linguistic phenomena. The hysteric evokes ontological uncertainty, the terror that "behind the multiple layers of masks there is nothing; or, at the most, nothing but the shapeless, mucous stuff of the life-substance" (Žižek, *The Metastases of Enjoyment* 150). Yet we cannot look away, for, by its very constitution, the symptom implies the field of language and presupposes an interlocutor: the hysteric coerces the witness to get involved in the plot, and retroactively confer meaning to a staging where the agent of an action was also its object.

In this introductory chapter I catalogue psychoanalytic appraisals of hysteria and its wider significance as *aesthesis*—lived experience not solely mediated by intellection, which is, however, not entirely resistant to conceptualization. I chose to begin with an extreme example of the post-structuralist prioritization of non-identity over identity—writing like a dog. My interpretation of hysteria, as summarized in the following claims, evokes familiar Deleuzian themes: hysteria deterritorializes the very language that it seeks deliverance in and supplants transcendental logic with a logic of multiplicities; it disinvests the body of fantasies of cohesion, language of stratification, and dialectics of narcissistic projection. But, if hysteria performs a critique of identity, and gives full play to its irreducible contradictions, it does not completely relinquish the subjective principle, and this is where it humanizes the impossible Deleuzian ideal. Rather, hysteria chooses what Adorno insists is the only option for the modern subject—it uses "the force of the subject to break through the deception of constitutive subjectivity" (*Negative Dialectics* xx). Hysterical identity is predicated on and presupposed by moments of non-identity, not eradicated by them: hysteria is in fact a prolepsis of identity that reveals identity to be nothing but prolepsis.

"There is aesthetics because there is art," I hear Jacques Rancière stating (*From an Aesthetic Point of View* 13), only to argue against the colonization of aesthetics by art. It is important that I clarify my use of the term "aesthetics," if I am to use it to describe not just (hysterical) narrative and art, but a more insidious hysteria of the signifier. Allow me a brief digression. If hysteria inspired the surrealism of Aragon and Breton, in the 90s it seems to have been reappraised to masquerade speciousness as substance. A few years ago, a label called "Hysteric Glamour" arrived on the sake-and-dance music-soaked catwalks of Tokyo. Fashionistas call its merchandise "terminally cute," roughly translated as that which is so cute that it is not cute at all, but knowing, ironical, and political. This brand of philosophical, if playful, activism, the same fashionistas warn, is a big no-no for anyone a day over thirty. An examination of literary representations of hysteria must, at some level, equate style and proliferating surface with substance, but while I draw attention to a lasting cultural fascination with hysterical performance and play, I also question the robust hermeneutic disgust of hysteria catalogued by the history of psychoanalysis. In this study hysteria is read as phenomenology *and* pathology. Hysteria has been associated for too long with a certain obdurate, debased materiality: this project is not about valorizing the (hysterical) body over its deconstruction in language. As I show in the following chapters, the corporeal body in hysteria has less substantial density than the body of language which surfaces in its lesions and breakdowns. I would like to say, as Maud Ellmann does of her book, *The Hunger Artists*, that this study is "concerned with *dis*embodiment, not bodies" (4): the text follows the misadventures of metaphors, to borrow another phrase from Ellmann, or of the symbolic displacements of hysteria as metaphor.[1] I am also deeply ambivalent about projects that seek to reclaim hysteria for identity-mongering on behalf of disarticulated and displaced peoples. As a diasporic intellectual seeking a foothold in the Anglo-American academy, I see no merit in speaking in mangled tongues, cultivating a nervous disposition, or maintaining a permanent breach between the signifier and the signified in speech-act situations—definitely not recommendable for anyone a day over thirty.

William James, in his 1896 lectures, defined hysteria as the "hyperaesthetic" disorder (Taylor 60). Aesthetics in this usage is much more than sensory cognition, or the sensory cognition of art: it can be placed in the tradition of Adorno, to signify, in the words of Martin Jay, "a certain type of relation between subject and object" (*The Dialectical Imagination* 66).

According to Kant, the aesthetic is a distinct faculty of 'non-conceptual' or indeterminate judgment, which brings together sensibility, understanding, and reason. This cognitive indeterminacy or ambiguity in the aesthetic sphere has inspired alternative formulations of the philosophical project. As Peter Osborne states in the introduction to *From an Aesthetic Point of View*,

> Hermeneutics, dialectical logic, Nietzschean affirmation, negative dialectic, deconstruction, a Lyotardian thinking of 'the event', and even Deleuzian materialism, all take their cue, in one way or another, from Kant's conception of a judgement which is reflective and undetermining in its logical form. 'Continental' philosophy, one might say, views the world from an aesthetic point of view. (4–5)

Osborne's book project evolved out of a conference at Middlesex University entitled "Where Theory Ends, There Art Begins," a modernization, he explains, of Friedrich Schlegel's aphorism, "Where philosophy ceases literature must begin." A contemplation of hysteria as an aesthetic must also begin with the limits of philosophy, and in the ruins of theory. Hysteria as a literary trope or artistic sensibility initiates a negative dialectics between abstraction and reality, and prompts a reflection on the limitation of knowledge. It uses discursivity to go beyond discursivity, "concepts to pry open . . . [what] cannot be accommodated by concepts," as Adorno stated in *Notes to Literature* (28). The nonconceptual in question is the (fleeting) object of hysterical desire, the thing itself, the indigent particular that inspires art; it is my argument that hysteria subscribes to a philosophy that remains committed to leaving this object nonidentical to itself.

I. LACAN'S HYSTERIA

Hysteria is both a disease, a nosological entity, with its own unspeakable or unspoken agonies, and a stifled language, which tries to recover the ineffable in pathological signs. The semiotics of hysteria baffle interpretive effort because of its paradoxical nature: hysteria's claims seem to be both somatogenic and psychogenic, it is both incommunicably private and spectacularly public, ambiguously signifying desire and disgust, "a category without content," as G. S. Rousseau states, while also possessing "an amorphous content incapable of being controlled by a clear category" (*Hysteria Beyond Freud* 93). Roy Porter eloquently reflects on the epistemological uncertainty that the historian of hysteria must grapple with:

is it a veritable joker in the taxonomic pack, a promiscuous diagnostic fly-by-night, never faithfully wedded to an authentic malady—or worse, a wholly spurious entity, a fancy-free disease name [. . .] independent of any corresponding disease-thing, a cover-up for medical ignorance? (*Hysteria Beyond Freud* 226)

Is hysteria a disease of the imagination, a mess of images and rogue ideas? Or is it only too real and yet undiagnosed? Is the female hysteric a madwoman or an actress? These and other questions shaped and deconstructed the politics of medicine, the protocols of culture, and the stylistics of literature, which have, from Hippocratic times, been complicitous in seeking to define and institutionalize the hysteric's reality. Hysterical (non)signification perplexes understanding in its unsteady shuffling between seeming and being. One is reminded of Adorno's description of art beauty, where he cites the ephemeral yet unforgettable phenomenon of fireworks as prototypical for artworks. As he states, "They appear empirically yet are liberated from the burden of the empirical, which is the obligation of duration; they are a sign from heaven yet artefactual, an ominous warning, a script that flashes up, vanishes, and indeed cannot be read for its meaning" (*Aesthetic Theory* 81). The theatre of suffering that hysteria performs in language alienates it from itself; to adopt Adorno's position of bemused spectatorship again, the glittering, artefactual moments of hysteria "are not only the other of the empirical world: Everything in them becomes other" (81).

Definitions of hysteria suffer from the excesses of the disorder itself. A full-frontal attack is impossible on this category with shifting contents. Its Protean ability to mimic the symptoms of other diseases has prompted some historiographers to call it a "Zeitgeist" disease, where every society has its particular contemporary disorders darkly mirrored in hysteria. To briefly consider an example, in the eighteenth century, the gendered language of medicine assigned hysteria to women, and rerouted unmanageable nervous disorders in men towards the symptom pool of hypochondria. By 1873, however, we have the term "neurasthenia" in America, which not only legitimized hysterical innervations in men, but also valorized them as hallmarks of evolutionary progress, signifying superior brain force and exquisitely refined sensibilities. Not surprisingly, the ranks of neurasthenics swelled, while hypochondria fell into disfavor. Writing of what she identifies as contemporary hysterical epidemics, Elaine Showalter says:

patients learn about diseases from the media, unconsciously develop the symptoms, and then attract media attention in an endless cycle. The

human imagination is not infinite, and we are all bombarded by these
plot lines every day. Inevitably, we all live out the social stories of our
time. (*Hystories* 6)

We are not all hysterical, at least not always, and what Showalter means by
this generalization is that hysteria provides us nevertheless with a linguistic
matrix where what is foreclosed in the socio-symbolic can nevertheless be ver-
balized, experienced, or enjoyed. The hysterical narrative has value not necessarily because it refers to a primordial truth, whether in organic or psychic
disease, trauma or the fantasy of trauma, but because it stands for a complex,
prohibited, yet sometimes predictable negotiation or contestation between the
subject and his or her milieu. Imagination is not infinite, Showalter states, so
we collectively inhabit the gray area between law and *jouissance* and iconically
express in "hystories" what is denied in social communication.

The hysteric both says too much and can't say enough. [In hysteria,
an idea becomes pathogenic because it is experienced in a psychic, unconscious state occluded by the ego.]The ego prevents this unconscious idea
from becoming conscious and surfacing in language, and a somatic defence is
formed. The vast set of physical, verbal, or gestural symptoms associated with
the disorder—stutters, seizures, coughs, paralyses, enervation, hyperactiv-
ity—reenacts a scene which, as Monique David-Ménard theorizes, "has never
been elaborated in language" (28). To illustrate her point David-Ménard cites
Freud's case history of Elisabeth von R. in *Studies on Hysteria* (1895). Elisabeth
felt stabs of pain each time Freud aroused a memory by a question. The pain
persisted for the duration of the recall, and disappeared when she finally mas-
tered it. What is interesting in Freud's elaboration of this coincidence is that
he no longer presumes a causal relation between the physiological symptom
and its psychic history, but sees the (bodily) pain coexisting homogeneously
with an unspeakable (psychic) pleasure. The pain, in fact, perversely, and con-
tinuously, speaks of the pleasure that has been revived in the symptom. The
hysterical symptom is over-determined yet unnarratable, and this, in turn,
binds the hysteric to the analyst, the subject-supposed-to-know, as also to the
discourse of the historian, the critic, and the student of literature.

Freud famously compared hysterical narratives to "an unnavigable river
whose stream is at one moment choked by masses of rock and at another
divided and lost among shallows and sandbanks" (SE 2: 160–61). The stories
he heard were riddled and raddled, and Freud chose a position from which
he had no choice but to provide a consistent and unbroken case history:
"Once we have discovered the concealed motives, which have often remained
unconscious, and have taken them into account, nothing that is puzzling

or contrary to rule remains in hysterical connections of thought, any more than in normal ones" (161). Freud's compulsion to mediate or hypostatize narratives, and attenuate the pain or obscene pleasure of his patients should be seen against his perfection of the psychoanalytic method and subsequent discoveries of the unconscious, repression, transference, telepathy, and resistance. Psychoanalysis was thought up as an indispensable paradigm for interventions in hysteria, whether objectivist, scientific, or aesthetic.

Freud was a student of Jean-Martin Charcot, the French clinical neurologist, who theatricalized phases and facets of hysteria during the 1860s and 1870s through his hysteria shows at the Salpêtrière. Charcot brilliantly systematized the symptomatology, stages, and diagnoses of hysteria, but as Mark S. Micale points out, his "achievements were medico-scientific and not therapeutic. Believing hysteria to be constitutional and degenerate, he held out little hope for its cure" (25). Freud used Charcot's neurological analyses to construct a psychological model of nervous illness that situated the psyche at the juncture of the body and discourse. The psychoanalytic method evolved as Freud tried to desublimate the rich and strange symptoms of his patients in the analytic question in a series of essays, the most controversial of which are *Studies on Hysteria* (co-authored with Josef Breuer, 1894) and *Fragment of an Analysis of a Case of Hysteria* (the "Dora" case, 1901). "Hysterics suffer mainly from reminiscences," Freud postulated in *Studies on Hysteria,* and went on to explain how painful memories in the distant past of the hysteric, where libido and disgust are associatively and agonistically linked, are incapable of articulating themselves. In the Freudian reconceptualization of hysteria, the "hysterical body thinks," says Monique David-Ménard; "a thought, which is initially psychical becomes a physiological mechanism without ceasing to be thought" (13). The beyond of language—heterogeneous fragments that cut and split the signifier—gets converted into bodily innervations: intense libidinal urges manifest themselves in signs of disgust. Freud held that the repressed memories were those of childhood sexual trauma, but rejected the seduction theory in 1897 to claim instead that the traumatic core was actually a realm of satisfaction that dared not speak its name. The hysteric, Freud diagnosed, denies the distinction between the phantasmatic and the real, and remains fixated in his or her demand for the (unreal) object of desire, stubbornly refusing to represent it, for every act of signification kills the thing itself and acknowledges lack. He or she is also inhibited in the choice of a sexual object, for no reality measures up to the perfection of phantasmatic representation. Believing that the repressed material had to be reintegrated in the conscious mental life of the patient, Freud proposed the psychoanalytic method. The apparatus Freud experimented with in order to cure his patients was electrical at first, but he successively used hypnosis, the templar pressure technique, and finally, the technique of free-association. The free-associative method is "unique to psychoanalysis," as Mark Micale points out, and consists of a "kind of attentive listening in which the wandering thoughts of the patient reveal unconscious psychic images and structures to the therapist" (28). Freud thus redirected the somaticist orientation of the discourse surrounding hysteria to a mentalist one, inspiring medical and cultural epistemes of the nervous body that sought to access asymptotically through language that which seemed insignifiable in it. He invested language—as theory and therapy—rather than medicine with the power to express and alleviate hysteria's agony. It was Lacan, however, who fully explored the potential of the work of the unconscious in speech.

When Jacques Lacan spoke of a "return to Freud" he had in mind the pre-1905 Freud, passionate about the interpretation of dreams, cuts and slips of language, the connection between symptom and speech, and not yet concerned with grounding his vision of the psyche in biology. To Freudian dogma Lacan brought to bear the linguistics of Roman Jakobson, the anthropology of Claude Lévi-Strauss, and the nightmares of the Surrealists. Lacan put a spin on the Oedipus complex by showing how the disconnection from the mother, and the entropic fragmentedness of the infant's experience of her body demonstrate "a certain dehiscence at the heart of the organism, a primordial Discord" (*Écrits* 4). This gap fosters Desire, unslakable and "eternally stretching forth towards the *desire for something else*" (*Écrits* 167). According to Lacan, this existential quest takes place in the context of the "Discourse of the Other" (*Écrits* 284), the symbolizing function of language which regulates and socializes desire, and plies it with a string of object-causes which give it nourishment and body. Without language there is no presupposition or representation of desire: I fix the shimmering, oscillating ego by submitting to the Other, the splitting function of language, and become a (divided) subject, a being (of alienation). Yet language cannot articulate desire, for it is in the interstice between the signifier and the signified that "what we call desire crawls, slips, escapes, like a ferret" (*Four Fundamental Concepts* 214).

Lacan's analysis of hysterical desire develops organically from his theorization of desire. He discredits the self-identity that is supposed of the ego in Freudian theory, and recasts it in a Hegelian mode, as the misadventures of identification undertaken by the subject. He thus repudiates reductive naturalist-determinist foundations, and traces the presence of conflicting libidinal and destructive forces in human relationships to the ontological instability of the ego, to its fundamental estrangement, or what Peter Dews calls "being-other" (58). Lacan envisions history as Hegelian, "the history of desired Desires"

(Kojève 6). Desirability becomes the primary trait of objects, overwhelming any "intrinsic" quality whatsoever, as a result of which objects become exchangeable: "What makes the human world a world covered with objects," says Lacan, "is grounded in the fact that the object of human interest is the object of desire of the other" (*The Pyschoses* 50). But if Lacan seems to echo the Hegelian discourse on desire, he also achieves a thorough revision of the *Phenomenology*. For Lacan, desire does not thematize human rationality, but springs in the aporia of rationality. The subject is not an agent or scenarist of his own desire, but alienated by the discourse of the Other, the unconscious.

> The promotion of consciousness as being essential to the subject in the historical after-effects of the Cartesian *cogito* is for me the deceptive accentuation of the transparency of the "I" in action at the expense of the opacity of the signifier that determines the "I." (*Écrits* 307)

Far from being a linguistic idealist who fetishizes the symbolic "as a kind of meta-subject" (Dews 77), Lacan bemoans the inadequacy of whatever is proffered in reply to our demand. Before he begins to speak, the subject is ontologically positioned in nothingness, with a plurality of signifiers around it, which immerse it in an Other. In order to be recognized, in order simply to *be*, the subject wields these signifiers, yet none of them is capable of representing him. Speaking is equivalent to "fading," into the unconscious, or the nonmeaning of the Other.

There is a little gain in this devastating rite of passage, namely the *objet petit a*. Object *a* is the symbol of a lack, a remainder of something from which the subject has separated itself, and a trace of the subject's persistent efforts at self-representation. It is the impossible, non-specularizable, paradoxical coalescence of the subject and its absolute other, defined as a lack: as Lacan stated, "the subject sees himself caused as a lack by *a*" (*Four Fundamental Concepts* 270). It is an absent cause, a lack that congeals subjectivity. An uncanny double of the subject, the object is the subject in the mode of objectivity. Žižek eloquently describes it as "the negative of the subject, a piece of flesh that the subject has to lose if he is to emerge as the void of the distance towards every objectivity" (*Supposing the Subject* 103). It cannot be subjectivized, enmeshed in consciousness, or projected as a specular double, only missed repeatedly in the subject's attempts at self-representation. Voice and gaze, which are extremely difficult to formalize or symbolize, can be said to perform the *objet a* function. Voice, for instance, is what lingers after the enunciating instance, and stands for something in another that is more than a sum of his parts. Gaze too—"there is something in the way you look at me"—cannot be signified readily. The look that falls from the other, and causes my desire, is not one that bestows recognition or validation of my returning look. The subject of Lacanian theory seeks this impossibility—this eye wide shut in its own enjoyment—and emerges as the effect of this impossible and unreciprocated desire.

The *objet a* belongs to the register of what Lacan calls the real, plenitude that lacks lack, and cannot be colonized by the imaginary-symbolic consciousness. The letter tries in vain to rend and differentiate its corpus, to overwrite and write it off through representation. The real is the ultimate gap in theory, something that persists "in a shadow, and dissolves itself as soon as we try to grasp it in its positive nature" (Žižek, "Grimaces of the Real" 169). In hysteria, the *objet a* appears in the position of the truth, enabling the hysteric to imagine the desert of the real in the symbolic. The truth of the hysteric's discourse is the real: the signifier is not all powerful in the hysteric structure, which makes for, in the words of Bruce Fink, "a unique configuration with respect to knowledge" (124). The hysteric questions the law and the paternal metaphor. As Fink notes:

> The hysteric pushes the master—incarnated in a partner, teacher, or whomever—to the point where he or she can find the master's knowledge lacking. [. . .] In addressing the master, the hysteric demands that he or she produce knowledge and then goes on to disprove his or her theories. (134)

The hysteric is clearly interested in something that is not fulfillment. Desire in hysteria is a desire for privation, for an unsatisfiable desire. The hysteric is every man or woman in the sense that he or she seeks from the Other what the Other does not have. Lacan himself called history (*histoire*) "*hystoire*" implying that every story has hysterical potential. The hysteric, however, has a strategy for sustaining her desire as unsatisfied. As Lacan said in *Ecrits,* she or he slips away as object: "desire is maintained only through the lack of satisfaction that is introduced into it when he eludes himself as object" (321). The hysteric creates a lack in the partner: she fades and vanishes as a subject, refusing to be the cause of the Other's *jouissance.* She reveals, as Ellie Ragland-Sullivan states, "the incapacity of any human subject to satisfy the ideals of Symbolic identifications" (*Feminism and Psychoanalysis* 164). The flashing question impersonated by hysteria—"Who am I, and what do I want?"—is, in inversion, its most substantive definition: the hysteric is being as nothing, a void in the place of the object, a being of lack, and what she wants is the lack of desire, not its cause.

Ironically, the hysteric in Freudian-Lacanian theory becomes a poster-child for negativity, though she stands for the opposite, a denial of negation. Freud, in his essay "Negation" said that there is no "no" in the unconscious, and the hysteric aspires for the plenitude promised by "the creation of the symbol of negation" (217). Lacan probably did not *see* the dynamic antinomies animating the hysteric because he was *listening* instead. What he could not confront in analysis was that the hysterical *body* thinks. David-Ménard frames this paradox in a question: "How can a thought be diverted into bodily innervation while at the same time it remains a thought—given that the hysterical symptom takes the place of an utterance?" (13) The logic of this corporeal thinking (without language) cannot be grasped by simply relegating the hysterical body to the realm of signs, where every innervation is a linguistic phenomenon. The hysterical body is the toad in Lacan's theoretical garden, an anthropomorphosis of a "gap in consciousness" (SE9: 234), a palpable absence not completely recuperable in analysis. In a different context, Terry Eagleton talks about the aesthetic as "the body's long inarticulate rebellion against the tyranny of the theoretical": according to Eagleton, "the aesthetic concerns this most gross and palpable dimension of the human, which post-Cartesian philosophy, in some curious lapse of attention, has somehow managed to overlook" (12). Hysteria too is an aesthetic that causes theoretical confusion through the undecidability between subject and object, though we cannot talk about the "body" too sanguinely in conjunction with it. The hysterical body is unnatural, a master of signifiers, and possessed with an abstract materiality which thwarts the stream of exposition and resists repression or sublation (*Aufhebung*). Its corpus can be likened to postmodern "metabooks" which, according to Fredric Jameson, "cannibalize other books, metatexts which collate bits of other texts" (96) without epistemophiliac acquisitiveness, and giving the slip to univocal reference and reality all the while.

But Lacanian theory need not be the micrometer by which we measure hysterical *jouissance*. In fact, according to Lacan there is not much enjoyment in hysteria. Lacan's prototypical hysteric is Freud's patient, the butcher's wife. In this Freudian case study, elaborated in *The Interpretation of Dreams*, the patient has a dream in which she wants to throw a dinner party, but only has a slice of smoked salmon in her larder. She would go shopping if it were not a Sunday afternoon, when all the shops are closed. She wants to order supplies by phone, but the phone does not work. She thus has to forego her wish to give a dinner. Freud links the content of the patient's dream to her female friend, who likes salmon very much but abstains from eating it (Lacan goes so far as to say that salmon is the signifier of the friend's desire). Freud also sees the salmon as a substitution for caviar, which the butcher's wife covets, yet doggedly refuses. Is the salmon/caviar then a metaphor for unsatisfied desire? Freud seems to think so, and contextualizes this dream to show how caviar is a rare commodity, and therefore a naughty food, in the butcher's wife's economic milieu. For Lacan, however, the dream is not just about unsatisfied desire, but signifies *a desire for* unsatisfied desire. As he says of the butcher, "there's a man a woman could have nothing to complain about, a genital character" (*Écrits* 261). The witty hysteric's desire for caviar then is the desire of a woman "who has everything, and who rejects precisely that" (261). That is why, the answer to the question What does the butcher's wife want? is not caviar, for she also does not want it.

There lurks another character in this drama of the unconscious playing out in the dream: the dreamer's husband. The patient identifies with her friend in her desire for privation. But there is also another reason why she wants to *be* her friend. Her husband prefers voluptuous women, yet seems to like the friend, who is skinny. He is fulfilled in his relationship with his wife, yet wants something that can never satisfy him. The butcher's wife's dream of discontent is thus ultimately about a dual hysterical identification with her husband as Other, and with what the Other lacks/desires. In Lacan's reading of this paradigm, the hysteric comes *to be* in that void of the other's desire. She poses as the signifier of what her husband lacks, the symbol of lost *jouissance,* the phallus.

This dream of the abandoned supper has generated a huge body of exegetical literature. As Diana Fuss catalogues in *Identification Papers,*

> The butcher's wife has been read, alternately, as a feminine-identified heterosexual (Freud), a masculine-identified heterosexual (Lacan), a masculine-identified lesbian (Clèment), a maternal-identified infant (Chase), and a feminine-identified lesbian (Fuss). (31)

Each retelling of the tale challenges interpretive mastery, generates more narrative, and prolongs the act of reading. As Fuss states, "the critical desire for a readable and concise ending to the story of the butcher's wife [. . .] paradoxically defers closure and keeps the story open to further rereading" (32). This classic Freudian case study of hysteria replicates the structure of a hysterical narrative itself.

Lacan's joyless hysteric obviates *jouissance* by masterfully absenting herself subjectively in her relationships, and by rifling through fungible stand-ins and *petit* objects that can never pass muster for plugging up desire. She is a virtuoso of dispossession and a glutton for punishment: radically dissatisfied, split irrevocably from identity or a fundamental referent, and relentlessly addressing her impossible demands for (self) knowledge to master signifiers. In other words, she has a tenuous grasp on knowledge because she sacrifices *jouissance*. Discourse assumes the function of *objet a,* that which arouses desire. What Lacan cannot account for is how *objet a,* the surplus value of the symbolic—a residue of the real inassimilable by the symbolic—can be the symbolic itself in the hysteric's universe. It is a para-dox, "analogous to the paradoxes Kant formulated with regard to aesthetic judgment," says Monique David-Ménard: "finality without end, universal-ity without concept" (184). David-Ménard offers the explanation that in hysteria, language or knowledge does not necessarily have the function of proscribing *jouissance*. Noting the (Lacanian) fallacy of attempting to eluci-date the unknown represented by non-phallic *jouissance* through principles of masculine sexuality, she adds "what causes their [women's] desire is that language does not simply bring jouissance to a halt" (188). Enjoyment is kindled, not killed by the signifier. The hysterical symptom manages to symbolize desire without sublating the thing desired. David-Ménard uses the Freudian term *Darstellung* (presentification) to designate a presentation (*Vorstellung*) that is not a representation:

> The hysteric posits the object of her desire in the element of presence [. . .]. In hysterical symptoms and attacks, the subject uses plastic and figurative thought to try to achieve the presence of the desired object and to achieve a jouissance in which nothing will have to be repre-sented—that is, acknowledged as absent. (110–11)

We are of course talking about body language in the context of hysterical signification—"dyspnoea, *tussis nervosa,* aphonia, and possibly migraines, together with depression, hysterical unsociability, and a *taedium vitae* which was probably not entirely genuine," as Freud catalogued Dora's problems in the "Fragment" (SE 7:23). The overflow of libido that is *jouissance* flouts the inscription of discourse, and the cultural sanctions of the Symbolic, through organic symptoms of disgust. Disgust screams the validity of the hysteric's desublimated enjoyment, unsupported by an erotogenic body.

Let me return to Freud to explain how disgust becomes the instru-ment of hysterical (dis)figuration. In his "Project for a Scientific Psychol-ogy," Freud uses the language of energetics to conceptualize the body in its pursuit of desire. The organism moves in pursuit of different goals, seeking discharge (and finally the homeostasis of death), and evaluating its actions with the touchstones of pleasure and unpleasure. Monique David-Ménard's *Hysteria from Freud to Lacan* focuses on the motility and movement that produce a "hysterogenic" body, instead of an "erotogenic" one. The erotogenic body results from a sexualization that is completed in a normative fashion, when the subject has been successfully cathected and circumscribed by the symbolic order. The hysterogenic body is produced when the sexualization of the body cannot be historically determined, and the subject cannot be readily initiated into the order of sexual difference: "the hysteric has no body, for something in the history of her body could not be formulated, except in symptoms" (David-Ménard 66). Desire is radically contentless, so there is no cessation of movement in fulfillment, and the subject turns away from the ideal goal in symptoms of disgust. As Lacan suggests in the *Four Fundamental Concepts,*

> it is in the function in which the sexual object moves towards the side
> of reality and presents itself as a parcel of meat that there emerges that
> form of desexualization that is so obvious that it is called in the case of
> the hysteric a reaction of disgust (172).

A hysterical conversion takes place in which the drive seeks a perverse way of achieving its goal: motor explorations manifest themselves in the signifying medium of the hysterogenic body, which is a surrogate for the erotogenic one. Through the (non)signifying elaboration of the symptom, the hysteric returns and recapitulates to her prohibited and lost scene of pleasure. And thus the hysteric, who has no body, also has too much body, a strange hysterogenic prosthesis, which proclaims its will to pleasure and claims its pound of flesh.

II. FITS AND FIREWORKS

In *The Critique of Judgment* (1790) Immanuel Kant writes: "There is only one kind of ugliness which cannot be represented in accordance with nature without destroying all aesthetical satisfaction, and consequently artistic beauty, namely, that which excites *disgust*" (155). When Derrida chances upon this passage, nothing short of a spectacular deconstruction of Kant's transcendental idealism happens.[2] Derrida dismisses Kant's concept of negative pleasure—as in the feeling of the sublime—as the absolute other of the beautiful. Though the sublime wreaks havoc on the faculties, its negativity can be transubstantiated in art. Again, though repulsive at first sight, the ugly, the unpleasant, the monstrous can be reclaimed and made beautiful: "the evil, the horrible, the negative in general are therefore not unassimilable to the system" (22). Only a single "thing" is:

> It will therefore form the transcendental of the transcendental, the
> non-transcendentalisable, the non-idealisable, and that is the *disgust-*
> *ing*. It presents itself, in the Kantian discourse, as a "species" (Art) of
> the hideous or of the hateful, but one quickly observes that it is not a
> species that would peacefully belong to its genus [. . .] it is no longer
> a question here of one of those negative values, one of those ugly or
> harmful things that art can represent and thereby idealize. The abso-
> lute excluded [*l'exclu absolu*] does not allow itself even to be granted
> the status of an object of negative pleasure or of ugliness redeemed by
> representation. (22)

It is the disgusting, unnameable in its alterity, that halts *economimesis* in its
processes—"in-sensible and un-intelligible, irrepresentable and unnameable,
[it is] the absolute other of the system" (22). Representation annuls itself in
too much enjoyment: as Derrida says, vomit "irresistibly forces one to con-
sume, but without allowing any chance for idealisation" (22). And, according
to Kant, the disgusting cannot be categorized as beautiful precisely because
it obliterates the difference between pure taste and actual tasting. It is like
the desire to vomit, forcing relief even as one strives against it. "The artistic
presentation of the object is no longer distinguished from the nature of the
object itself in our sensation, and thus it is impossible that it can be regarded
as beautiful," states Kant ("Economimesis," 22). But as Derrida inquires,
"Would not disgust, by turning itself back against actual tasting, also be the
origin of pure taste, in the wake of a sort of catastrophe?" (16). Derrida questions the conceptual logic of Kantian aesthetics by pointing to an excrescence—vomit—that shatters the unity of its ideality. The parergonal overflow
is a heterogeneity, which "does not allow itself to be digested, or represented,
or stated," and which, "by never letting itself be swallowed must therefore
cause itself to be vomited" (21). If the disgusting is the other of the beautiful,
it is also an uncanny double, which too refuses to be consumed, and is, in
Isobel Armstrong's Adornian commentary, "a promise of the as yet unsayable,
a fleeting promise of new possibilities, of scarcely envisioned openings in
experience emancipated from the world of exchange" ("And Beauty?" 279).
Beauty is not a thing, but a want—like disgust, it seeks to defer consummation through, to quote Armstrong again, "unstillable yearning" (279).

Derrida inscribes the perfunctory opposition of taste/disgust in the
mouth, which speaks and eats, consumes ideally and literally, and represents
the logocentric (expressive) system as well as that which it cannot include
(vomitive): "the split between all the values that at one moment or another
are opposed will pass through the mouth: what it finds good or what it finds

bad, according to what is sensible or ideal . . ." (16). Derridean theory makes Kantian aesthetics crassly spit out what displeases it, and what it cannot ravenously absorb: the excremental body and animalistic enjoyment of the senses. The objectal remainder of consuming orality, an urge to vomit where an appetite for incorporation turns into in an aversion toward incorporation, is the hysteric aesthetic. To comprehend it, one would have to decode the epistemology of disgust, which, Ned Lukacher asserts, is at the heart of the conversion symptom in hysteria: "The epistemology of the movement of disgust is the epistemology of the tropological substitutions that describe the language of hysterical speech and of the hysterical body."[3] Libidinal, psychical pleasure, on account of its inadmissibility into the symbolic, speaks through symptoms of organic, physical disgust. Through the (non)signifying elaboration of the symptom, the hysteric secures a sublimatory hold over his or her prohibited and lost scene of pleasure. Sexual disgust is a passionate disavowal, symptomatically proclaiming a desire that persists only as unfulfilled. The hysteric is a truly beautiful soul in that she inhabits a world "where consumption does not dominate, even if we give this world no content" (Armstrong 281).

The defining argument of this book is that hysteria is an aesthetics of disgust, a mode of aesthetic reception whose terms of exegesis and enjoyment are revulsion, consternation, and hermetic enervation. Disgust, of course, is the new black for the culture vultures of the nineties and noughties, as a brief foray into the millennial mood of the British Art scene would reveal. What else would you don when viewing sculptor Mark Quinn's "Self," shown as part of the Sensation exhibition at the Royal Academy, and consisting of a mould of his head into which he had poured eight pints of his own blood? Or Mona Hatoum's "Corps Etranger," video images of the interior of her body, filmed through every orifice with a surgeon's endoscopic camera, and projected on to the floor of the gallery (Edinburgh Festival, 1998)? Waist-high heaps of flowers for Diana were decaying on the park lawns in front of Kensington Palace when an exhibition presciently called "Sensation" opened in the Royal Academy on September 18, 1997. It featured 120 works by 42 artists from different London art schools who burst into the scene nearly ten years ago when Damien Hirst staged a tripartite student exhibition, "Freeze." The "Freeze" artists—Fiona Rae, Jennie Saville, Rachel Whiteread, Jake and Dinos Chapman, Marc Quinn, Sarah Lucas, to name a few—named after Hirst's cow-and-formaldehyde piece, represented unruly, body-obsessed, dysfunctional, bleeding-edge contemporary art. "There will be works of art on display in the Sensation exhibition which some people may find distasteful," read the Royal Academy Press release. Despite vehement protests from children's rights groups about Marcus Harvey's portrait of child serial-killer Myra Hindley (done with children's handprints) and angry denunciations of Tracey Emin's "Everyone I Have Ever Slept With," a tent-like structure embroidered with names of her lovers, her brother, even a foetus that she aborted, and of Chris Ofili's elephant dung-encrusted painting of The Holy Virgin Mary, the show closed on 300,000 visitors.

Mayor Rudy Guiliani called Ofili's work "sick stuff" on the eve of the New York exhibition of "Sensation," and threatened the Brooklyn Museum of Art with a cancellation of its annual $7m City Hall grant: "The idea of having so-called works of art in which people are throwing elephant dung at a picture of the Virgin Mary is sick" ("Sensation Sparks New York Storm," BBC News online, 23 September, 1999). William A. Donohue, President of the Catholic League for Religious and Civil Rights, said, "it is designed to shock, but instead it induces revulsion." Hillary Rodham Clinton, who at the time was running for the US Senate against Guiliani, publicly declared that she would not got to see the exhibit, while also criticizing the city mayor's bullying of the Brooklyn Museum. A lawsuit (seeking a preliminary injunction against the city), PETA involvement (over a Damien Hirst piggy sliced nose to tail in formaldehyde), and a howl of outrage from the New York art scene later, Sensation opened at the Brooklyn Museum of Art on October 2, 1999. The Catholic League handed out vomit bags at the opening, loudly singing hymns and saying rosaries outside the museum.

Disgust is the new stick with which we beat ourselves even as we furtively inhabit and guiltily withdraw from the corpus of the disgusting. Will Self's *How the Dead Live* brilliantly captures the vicariousness that is integral to our enjoyment of disgust. It has as its protagonist the dead-alive Lily Bloom, coming to terms with the banal "deathaucracy" of London. She is not spiritualized in death, and is instead rebarbatively earthy: surrounding her are the calcified foetus she once miscarried, her little son killed by a lorry, the three eyeless "Fats" (her Fates), obese conglomerates of herself made of all the pounds she has put off and on again. Will Self ghost-writes about post-war Britain with loathing and nostalgia, his virtuoso punning and verbal tricks mnemosynistically scabbing over collective and private sores: it is pure, festering Self-disgust, achingly personal and furiously denied.

The list of pickled cows (Hirst), children with mutant genitalia (the Chapman brothers), Tracey Emin's dirty linen, Ben Okri's elephant dung— bric-à-brac which taught us the viability of disgust as an aesthetic response—is tediously long, but an instance of a more subtle and insidious form of disgust-mongering, under the aegis of art, would be the "Spectacular Bodies" show at the Hayward Gallery (19 October 2000–14 January 2001). Claiming to be an examination of "the Art and Science of the Human Body from Leonardo to Now," it pitches its wares to our inner anatomist-artist. Corpses can be recycled as art, and inspirational art at that, as evidenced in the array of Dutch 17th- and 18th-century group portraits of anatomists, posing with their cadavers in a compositional imitation of Christian nativity. The curio shop of science evokes appetency for knowledge and then nausea: Manfredini's life-size ceramics of expectant mothers peeling back their abdominal skin like the petals of a flower; William Pink's famous 1834 cast of the flayed body of a convicted smuggler, forced into the pose of the classical statue of "The Dying Gaul" before rigor set in; a decorated foetus in a jar, a ghoulish memento of 18th-century scientific callousness. "Body Worlds" is another hugely controversial exhibition by artist and anatomist Gunther von Hagens, which opened in March 2002 at the Atlantis Gallery in London. The Tory MP Teddy Taylor prophesied on Radio 4's Today program that: "This will only appeal to ghoulish groups in our society" (18/3/02). The anatomist preserves bodies using polymer chemistry, a preservation technique that replaces water in cells with plastic material to make the bodies rigid, odorless, and permanently preserved. This "event-anatomy" show features 175 body parts and 25 full human cadavers set in "artistic poses": a skinned corpse in an exhibitionist attitude with his epidermis slung across one arm, a flayed pregnant woman with her womb slashed to reveal a seven-month-old foetus, a skinless rider astride a skinless horse with his brain in his hand. Professor von Hagens has called on British art-lovers to donate their bodies to future exhibits of corpses posed to look as if they are engaged in recreational activities like chess. According to statistics provided by *The Guardian* (12/3/02), the show has a record of at least one fainting a day. When it went on display in Brussels, 5% of the Belgian population turned up. Around 50% left the exhibition looking gutted and resolved to improve their health. A further 10% quit smoking on the spot.

In summer 2000, the Heaven and Hell exhibition at the Royal Museum in Edinburgh showcased not only 6,000 years of global perspectives on death, but also a primordial shudder of abhorrence, a forceful eschewal of what we never could ingest. Tanya Wilson from *The Guardian* catalogued spirit guided-dogs and forks for eating human flesh with mixed feelings:

> brutal corpse collars, scary contraptions like modern-day bike locks, used to protect corpses from body-snatching. Standard-issue shrouds, all clinically white, non-toxic and fully-combustible (gulp) [. . .] ecologically friendly cardboard and wicker basket coffins—mmm, shuffle off this mortal coil in a giant picnic hamper . . . (Saturday Review, *The Guardian* 29/7/00)

Disgust is this catch in the throat, this inability to fully name and shame the vexed enjoyment of the forbidden and the useless. It is a fragment of what Lacan calls the real, a traumatic remainder or cause of the chain of signification that brings about the subject, "the object that cannot be swallowed, as it were, which remains stuck in the gullet of the signifier" (*The Four Fundamental Concepts* 270).

A theorization of disgust provides a valuable hermeneutic tool to understand the refusal of hermeneutics, and inadequacy of theory. Disgust speaks for the heterogeneous elements which disturb critical journeys or plunge them into heterotopias, which, as Iain Chambers states, "desiccate speech, stop words in their tracks, contest the very possibility of grammar at its source; they dissolve our myths and sterilize the lyricism of our sentences" (*Travellers' Tales* 245). Disgust inhabits a realm of contradiction, which could be likened to what Adorno called "the aporia of aesthetics" (*Aesthetic Theory* 72). According to Adorno, art imitates what is indeterminable in things: "Its object is determined negatively, as indeterminable. It is for this reason that art requires philosophy, which interprets it in order to say what it is unable to say, whereas art is only able to say it by not saying it" (72). The hysteric-aesthetic dis-figures its object, investing it with libido via disgust. I have mentioned earlier that hysterical signification resembles what Adorno called the magic of the aesthetic, as instanced in the phenomenon of fireworks. Adorno's theory of the aesthetic is very relevant to a theorization of the aesthetics of disgust because hysteria is an empirical happening, yet "liberated from the burden of the empirical" (81): like the artefactual reality of fireworks, it is, to quote Armstrong, a "magical phenomenon . . . an astonishment and a wonder, intellectual delight and kinaesthetic happening" ("And Beauty?" 275). Adorno uses another metaphor to describe the character of aesthetic experience: that of (male) orgasm. As Adorno claims in the following passage, "aesthetic experience resembles sexual experience, indeed its culmination":

> The way the beloved image is transformed in this experience, the way rigidification is unified with what is most intensely alive, effectively makes the experience the incarnated prototype of aesthetic experience. [. . .] Artworks synthesize ununifiable, nonidentical elements that grind away at each other; they truly seek the identity of the identical and the nonidentical processually because even their unity is only an element and not the magical formula of the whole. [. . .] This reciprocity constitutes art's dynamic; it is an irresolvable antithesis that is never brought to rest in the state of being. Artworks are such only *in actu* because their tension does not terminate in pure identity with either

extreme. [. . .] The movement of artworks must be at a standstill and thereby become visible. (*Aesthetic Theory* 176)

Aesthetic experience, according to Adorno, is processual and incessantly dynamic, shimmering between turgidity and paroxysmal resolution. Adorno here is conceptualizing a restless, antithetical process, which never comes to halt in static being, or brings the non-identical to expression. At best it is a halted motion, which remains visible *qua* motion in this standstill. It builds up to an explosive and vivid end, which is not just an end but also a beginning of another magical series of fireworks or orgasms. Aesthetic autonomy represses its sensual moment in this processual vanishing, drawing parallels with hysterical expressivity, which continually surmounts its bodily character.

For Adorno, the work of art is intrinsically material, yet escapes being a sum of its parts. It is undeniable that "artwork will die of its lack of the clown's red nose and grotesque devices, the fountain's upsurge, the musical comedy's svelte routine of sequin- and fish-netted legs high kicking in unison" (Armstrong 277–78). But art is still that shimmering instantiation, that substantial image that is incomparable to the mode and disparate materials of its production. The aesthetic is always "becoming actual," fusing the empirical with a countertendency to it: "a script that flashes up, vanishes, and indeed cannot be read for its meaning" (*Aesthetic Theory* 80). A genuine work of art plays on the existing to bring into being something that did not exist before: it creates what Adorno calls an "apparition," which compels us to contemplate the semblance of the non-existing. The object of art remains incommensurable to the mediation or intentionality that posits it: "It manifests foreignness at the same time that it seeks to make experiential what is thing-like and foreign" (*Aesthetic Theory* 84). Artworks have the immanence of a fleeting second, even when carved in stone, and impinge on the spectator's consciousness with the suddenness and evanescence of fireworks. They kindle thing and appearance for a short, spectacular duration, and resemble the Kantian thing, Adorno concedes, "as the transcendent thing-in-itself and as an object subjectively constituted through the law of its phenomena" (*Aesthetic Theory* 99). Art is awash with contradictory forces that curiously constitute its critical force. Its estrangement from its history, geography, and science, does not necessarily give it a perspective beyond them. If it exists solely for its own sake, it risks losing cultural value and political purchase. If, on the other hand, it exists to forward a cultural or political critique, its intervention is compromised by the form and content of the enunciation, which must belong to the symbolic economy to make sense as it were. Art can only succeed as a form of play, wresting a provisional referentiality from the equal and opposite forces of sense/concept and spirit/object.

Aesthetics, according to Adorno, is not applied philosophy, but rather in itself philosophical. It is "the intuition of what is not intuitable: it is akin to the conceptual without the concept" (96). Adorno demurs against Kant on the subject of art's so-called intuitability. In the *Critique of Judgment* Kant adumbrated that "[T]he beautiful is that which pleases universally without a concept" (as cited in *Aesthetic Theory* 94). If that were so, aesthetic experience would not require the labor of observation, couch potatoes would be venerated art critics, and art would be coterminous with its univocal "message": "Behind the cult of intuitability lurks the philistine convention of the body that lies stretched out on the sofa while the soul soars to the heights" (98). Art's sensuousness distinguishes it from theory, but it is at the same time discursive and non-sensuous enough to hold up as a sensuous *structure*. The shudder, which the apparition of every authentic artwork presupposes, destroys the universality of the ever-same with its particularity. Its symbols and metaphors are always skiving their referential function: art resists the empirical world, and the reification that would make it intuitable. It needs the language of concepts to express the nonconceptual. As Adorno puts it, "Art militates against the concept as much as it does against domination, but for this opposition, it, like philosophy, requires concepts" (*Aesthetic Theory* 96).

If, as Adorno claims, art requires philosophy, it must surely be a philosophy that conceptualizes the object in its particularity and heterogeneity without integrating it. Hegelian dialectics clearly wouldn't do here, for in it the other of thought is "reproduced in thought itself as its immanent contradiction" (*Negative Dialectics* 35). Traditional epistemology seems to necessitate the consumption of the object by the subject: to comprehend or represent the subaltern other is to sublate its contingent singularity in the immanence of the concept or subject. Adorno's idea of philosophical critique is revolutionary in that it does not involve a familiarizing of difference in identity. As Asha Varadharajan remarks, "Adorno celebrates the birth of thought at the very moment that it contemplates the dissolution of the concept (as well as of itself) in the recalcitrance of the object" (50). For him, the moment of radical uncertainty, when spirit boggles on matter it cannot define or abstract, is a definitive one of the "impossible possibility" of philosophy (*Prisms* 247). *Negative Dialectics* is exemplary of this philosophical method, written as it is around the realization that "objects do not go into their concepts without leaving a remainder" (5). The concept is made to take cognizance of the object without de-materializing it in a relationship of adequation. To think is not to identify, or subsume fact in category, but to gain an "insight into the constitutive character of the nonconceptual in the concept" (*Negative Dialectics* 12). Dialectical thinking is turned on its head in that it reflects not the integrity of the subject, but the fallacy of "mistaking its own image for concretion" (*Negative Dialectics* 13). Instead of solidly confronting each other, concept and object "reciprocally permeate each other" (*Negative Dialectics* 139). It is, however, important to note that Adorno's non-identity thinking does not completely abandon the principle of identity. While he criticizes Hegel's dialectic as being the most insidious form of identity thinking, and lyrically evokes images of a self claustrophobically trapped in its own immanence, Adorno's is—and I quote Peter Dews here—"a deeply dialectical sensibility" (*The Limits of Disenchantment*). As he says in *Negative Dialectics:*

> the ideal of identity must not simply be discarded. Living in the rebuke that the thing is not identical with the concept is the concept's longing to become identical with the thing. This is how the sense of non-identity contains identity. (149)

Adorno's negative dialectics exposes "the primal form of ideology" (Negative *Dialectics* 148) of the principle of identity. Its political dimension, as Asha Varadharajan notes, lies in its efforts to "reveal the contradictions within reality" by producing "a philosophy that sets itself up as a contradiction *against* reality" (64). Thought attempts to think against itself by cathecting with its somatic moment, and releasing sensuousness into being. This is not a return to the body and its pleasures—for Adorno, fascism "was the absolute sensation" (*Minima Moralia* 234)—but a mode of pitching discourse, as Eagleton says, "into a constant state of crisis . . . struggling in the structure of every sentence to avoid at once a 'bad' immediacy of the object and the false self-identity of the concept" (*The Ideology of the Aesthetic* 341). Philosophy should strain towards the ineluctable and inexpressible sensuousness that animates art, without ceasing to negate it through conceptualization. Theory will expunge itself if it tries to imitate art at the expense of systematic thought: it "can neither circumvent such negation nor submit to it. It must strive, by way of concept, to transcend the concept" (*Negative Dialectics* 15). What it can emulate from art is, in Eagleton's words, its "paratactic logicality" which may be said to represent "an arational reason confronting an irrational rationality" (351). If philosophy brings cogency to the play of the aesthetic, it also takes cognizance, in the artifact's pregnant silence, of what is unsayable by it.

I have been drawing parallels between Lacan and Adorno to finally pose the following question: is psychoanalysis to hysteria what (non-transcendental) philosophy is to the aesthetic? Lacan saw the hysterical symptom as "letters of suffering in the subject's flesh" (*Écrits* 92). Freud's master Charcot described himself as "*visuel,* a man who sees" (SE3:12), a spectator of production of non-sense and unreason in the hysteric's passionate attitudes. The hysteric's eternal questions are: What does the Other want? How do I stand with respect to this Other? However, it is impossible to know *through* whom and *for* whom she poses these questions. The hysteric captures the object—the object-cause of the trauma that gave rise to her malady, and to whom her desire is now addressed—in an elaborate intrigue. She needs the Other as an addressee but vehemently resists interpellation by another. Hysteria, says Žižek, "[is] the name for this stance of ambivalent fascination in the face of the object that terrifies and repels us" (*The Ticklish Subject* 249). Freud tells us, with regard to the Rat Man and his recital of the theme of his obsession, that of the rat forced into the victim's anus: "His face reflected the horror of a pleasure of which he was unaware" (*Standard Edition* 10, 167–68). This psychic dilemma in turn manifests itself in what Diana Fuss calls the "astonishing *mobility* and *plasticity* of hysterical identification" (115), which poses problems for the psychoanalyst trying to cure it.

Lacan calls Freud's technique of interpretation "the dialectic of the con-sciousness-of-self, as realized from Socrates to Hegel" (Ècrits 79-80). Freud saw the subject as de-centered, or as having a center other than consciousness. The aim of psychoanalysis was to unite the particular (consciousness) with the universal (unconscious). The task of the analyst is to bring down the language barrier—the wall of empty words—between him and the subject to introduce the latter to the "primary language" from which derives the symbolism of his symptoms, and wherein a universal language (langue) has perfect coincidence with the particularized idiolect of his desire. Psychoanalytic dialogue thus strives to be "a communication in which the sender [i.e., the subject] receives his own message back from the receiver [i.e., the analyst] in an inverted form" (85). Lacan is implying here that the speech of the subject presupposes its own reply: the lacunae among the spoken words are suffused with the subject's unconscious, and the analyst's role is to bring this unconscious dimension of the analysand's speech into his consciousness. The function of the analyst's language, Lacan cautions, is "not to inform but to evoke" (86), that is to evoke resonances, conscious and unconscious, in the subject's speech. Lacan comes closest to formulating the nature of the analyst's responsibility in the following statement: "if I call the person to whom I am speaking by whatever name I choose to give him, I intimate to him the subjective function that he will take on again in order to reply to me, even if it is to repudiate this function" (86–87). Lacan thus reorders the antinomies in the Freudian dialectic to favour object at the expense of the subject. It is the analyst's ethical duty to constitute his own subjectivity like a question, and seek in speech the response of the other: "In order to find him, I call him by a name that he must assume or refuse in order to reply to me" (italics mine, 86). The interchange of psychoanalytic dialogue is a communication in which the sender (the analysand) receives his own message back from the receiver (the analyst) "in an inverted form" (83).[4]

If, in the Freudian tradition, the analyst confers on the subject's speech its "dialectical punctuation" (95), Lacan strains to show that he is certainly not the master of the situation, since the dimension of the real enters into the psychoanalytic discourse: "the analyst's abstention, his refusal to reply, is an element of reality in analysis" (95). Lacan uses the word "reality" interchangeably with "real" to indicate an order that is neither symbolic nor imaginary—a place of no words, the stumbling block of all articulation, and the indivisible trace that lingers after it. The analyst is enjoined by Lacan to inhabit a junction between the symbolic and the real, a zone of "pure negativity" (95). It is in this resonating silence that the subject's full speech is articulated: it is through the preservation of distance between the psychoanalytic concept and its object that the Lacanian (negative) dialectic of recognition and misrecognition is set in motion.

Deleuze forewarned that a variation of language is produced when it ceases to be a homogeneous system in equilibrium, or near equilibrium. "If the system appears to be in perpetual disequilibrium, if the system bifurcates—and has terms each one of which traverses a zone of continuous variation—language itself will begin to vibrate and stutter" ("He Stuttered" 24). Hysteria ushers creativity in the regime of representational signs by making the language system stutter. The hysteric reclaims sense from the system that differentiates between sensation and sensibility, sound and language, bodies and propositions of bodies, eating and speaking. Letting the flesh of syntax slide off the bones of schematic determinacy, the hysteric writes with animal necessity and a foreigner's paranoid optimism.

Chapter Two

Too Much, Too Little: The Emotional Capital of Victorian Melodrama

Conducting a survey for London's *Evening Standard* magazine in December 1999, Matthew Baylis, ex-storyliner on *Eastenders*,[1] learned a thing or two apropos of the flagship show's "authenticity." Walford, E20, home to the soap East Londoners, is, of course, fictional, so Baylis headed for Walthamstow and Stratford, to experience the real thing. At Walthamstow Market, Linda Arnold, the market inspector, was dismissive of her *Eastenders* counterpart, Lisa Shaw. Lisa's leather trousers and immaculately coiffed hair were impossibly fancy for her job, she said witheringly. Others felt that the soap showcased abjection, drudgery, and stagnation, and that they therefore could not identify with the lifestyle depicted in it. As June, a keen but critical observer, pointed out scathingly about the TV characters: "They go to Southend for their holidays, live in grotty houses, and have the same old wallpaper for 12 years. People here aren't like that. I've got koi carp and a Japanese garden." When Baylis put his findings to a former director of the show, the latter defended the show's commitment to depicting quotidian realities: "People are sensitive when they see themselves on TV. To be fair, that's not always because the portrayal is inaccurate. Good TV is a mirror. We don't always like what we see in the mirror." Then, contradicting his previous statement, he argued that drama should not be enslaved to facts.

> If they get in the way—and that only happens five per cent of the time—we'll bend them. [. . .] It's important that the canvas is truthful—the settings and the jobs people do—but you have to play around with the paint to make something people want to see.

To give the people what they want, or to be true to its perception of the people's demands, while also outguessing and exceeding their imagination,

Eastenders deploys melodramatic tactics. Larger-than-life characters like the Mitchell brothers—homicidal mama's boy Grant and the sociopath Phil— the village gossip, police, and social worker Dot Cotton, the suave lady killer Steve Owen and the boy he framed, the crazed Matthew Rose, the fallen cop Beppe DeMarco, the sparkling and damaged child-woman Bianca Jackson, to name a few, lead lives overfraught with urban derangements. Even the show's hoipolloi, stock types like launderette bolshie Pauline Fowler, foxy pub lady Peggy Mitchell, local capitalist Ian Beale (of "Beale's Plaice" and "Beale's Market") or the endearing maladroit, Barry Evans, are impresarios of affect, completely at ease with heavily charged material. Physical and mental well being on Albert Square is as threatened by explosions, rapes, murders, and road accidents, as by asininity, petty jealousy, slander, perfidy, and malice. Horrible mishaps befall individual characters. Bianca has a malformed foetus because she had neglected to take her folic acid tablets in the first trimester. 'Tiff' narrowly escapes death in a domestic row, only to be run over by her mother-in-law's aged but frisky paramour, speeding to be with her on New Year's Eve. Carol is about to have a fifth child by a fifth partner, when it comes to her attention that he is sleeping with her firstborn, herself married with a child. The characters inflict horrible things on one another. The brothers Mitchell seem locked in a struggle unto death. Ian, whose daughter has a false cancer scare, seeks to capitalize on girlfriend Melanie's pity and sympathy, and inveigles her to the marriage altar with lies about a positive prognosis. As in melodrama, the good, bad, and the ugly are demarcated without uncertainty in the perceptual grid. The repressed returns inevitably, literally, and collects its due with interest, and life on the Square is impossible for the woman with a past. Ask Nina the reformed prostitute who is named and shamed eventually by a former client, or Louise, whose affair with her son-in-law catalyzes daughter Tiffany's untimely death. While secrets and hermeneutic enigmas propel the narrative and nucleate cliffhanger episodes, information is rarely withheld from the viewers. As the BBC trailer for *Eastenders* insists, "Everybody's talking about it," always. Our curiosity is whetted and sustained over substantial temporal gaps precisely because we know more than the dramatis personae, anticipate what is to come, and fear its incalculable impact. The surprising lure to identification lies not in the plausibility of plot and character, but in their delightful weightlessness, and in the dexterous production of a sublime continuum where polarities of response—the eastenders are both like us and unreal—are juxtaposed comfortably.

When I started writing this chapter, I had watched *Eastenders* on BBC 1 for three years already, nearly every Monday, Tuesday, and Thursday, and sometimes the Sunday Omnibus for missed or particularly delectable episodes. While

wishing for greater intellectual and emotional complexity in my staple entertainment than that provided by a series that lingers voyeuristically on Viagra-fuelled
marriages and Viagra-fuelled adulteries, I find myself compulsively going back
for more. If this TV drama is junk, it appears that the fifteen million that view
each episode of the show can gorge themselves silly on it. Through the lens of
this peculiar attachment to *Eastenders,* I see the nineteenth-century fascination
with melodrama too as a sort of national bulimia, and the socio-politico-cul-
tural exigencies of the time as promoting this form of inconspicuous consumption. In this chapter, I wish to contextualize and analyze two nineteenth-century
melodramas (as both stage dramas and literary texts), much unlike each other
in form and content—political, social, and artistic—the composition of their
respective theatrical audiences, and produced more than eighty years apart.
Ranging over a hundred years of theatrical history, they are two very different paradigms for studying Victorian melodrama as a localized ethnography of
bourgeois and proletariat cultural formation. If the play from 1893, *The Second
Mrs Tanqueray,* is melodrama's confident, erudite ego, the 1829 nautical melodrama, *Black Ey'd Susan,* is its id, messy with unresolved conflict, and repressed.
I use these primary texts to try to elucidate the melodramatic as an aesthetic and
an alternative discourse, which supplements sense with mixed and tumultuous
sensations, and occasionally reduces the former to a spectre.

I start with a discussion of the features of Victorian melodrama, looking
at its phenomenological pleasure-body and the discursive structure that seeks,
in vain, to regulate the pittance of pleasure allowed to it. I wish to show that
melodrama is split by language in a way that does not subjugate it to what
Lacan calls the phallic function, or the alienation brought about by the symbolic register. At the vortex of the unstable order and hysteria of identities in
melodrama is a lack that cannot be dialectized or pervaded by signifiers. My
reading of melodrama ultimately falls into that aporia: I conclude that our
appreciation of the endless intensity of the genre is ultimately unpronounce-
able, a metaphorical lump in the throat. The psychoanalytic method lends
support to the historicist project by emphasizing the traffic between fantasy
and fact, unconscious and conscious thought, repression and expression, disgust and desire, melodramatic excess and lack. The "world which is escaped
into," structured by the unreal conflicts and solutions of melodrama, is seen
to have causal and phantasmal links with the "world which is escaped from,"
a microcosm rocked by unsettling political and economical change, and epistemological discovery (*English Drama* 247).

The world of Victorian melodrama is of course as if epistemically constructed by fantasy; plot and meaning are elaborated sensationally and spectacularly, ratiocination follows the laws of the heart, not head, the tragic or

pathetic are syncopated by flashes of the comic, characters are intelligible, if not wholly identifiable, the question of morality is not impossible or divided against itself, action and situation are domesticated and picturesque, and there is musical accompaniment. What it lacks in intellectual heft, profound or abstract philosophy, or self-deprecatory humor, it makes up for in its inexpedient, relaxing and feel-good effects. This brand of dramaLite aids perception, espouses recognition, and collaborates with the audience to enjoy an artifact, and inhabit a fantasy. As Martin Meisel states,

> despite an affective climate of danger, anxiety and impasse, despite an exposure to the buffeting of violent sensations, abrupt discontinuities, and deliberately evoked misapprehension, most melodrama carries with it an assurance of reassurance, of obscurities dispelled, ambiguities resolved, of a vigorously marked binary pattern of coherence. ("Scattered Chiaroscuro" 67)

Melodrama is a "pictorial dramaturgy" (Meisel, "Speaking Pictures" 54) that seeks to commute the most intractable realities in the channel of visual perception: natural calamities, supernatural occurrences, or occulted mental states. Action is often dissipated in extravagant effects, and narrative situations are encapsulated in the motionless expressiveness of tableau for maximum dramatic impact. One such legible concretion of meaning can be seen in Tom Taylor and Charles Reade's *Masks and Faces* (1852). Peg Woffington is the femme fatale in the play; the traditional scapegoat of domestic melodrama, as also its super-ego like consciousness, she is an exemplar of melodramatic expressivity. In a poignant scene, Woffington literally lends her face to the canvas of an admiring painter, pretending to be her own portrait. Her face in the picture frame silently serves as a double representation, underscoring the politics of the play. She mimics or somatizes a (phantom, or aesthetic) replica of herself (lovingly painted and then petulantly destroyed by Triplet), in itself a representation or approximation, thereby pointing to the constructed, iterative nature of her burlesque-like identity. The naked face does the work of a mask, nature stands in for art; yet, Peg Woffington wants the wronged wife, Mabel Vane, to know that though the face (of a woman) seems contiguous with the mask (of an actress), it is also anterior to it, and can rend it at will. "Ah!—a tear! it is alive"(163), cries out Mabel Vane as the supposed picture melts in front of her eyes. The ambivalences at the heart of identity formation constitute the contingent traumatism of melodrama, a passion that plays out in non-verbal integers. Peg Woffington's face stages a pantomime of symptoms under the scrutiny of her moral adversary, the virtuous wife alternating between pride, sexual power, self-division, and pain. She is the very ground of representation, acting out identifications, reliving various roles. She is Peg Woffington and Mabel Vane, the masks we wear, and the nakedness beneath. Melodrama does prioritize a patriarchal stereotyping of femininity where the "woman" function integrates itself into the symbolic only through a structural or hysterical splitting. What it also inevitably illustrates, perhaps unwittingly, is that there is no primordial substance that is anterior or superior to the symbolic "mask"; subjectivity itself persists as nothingness, robbed of its ontological gel through the overblown inconsistencies of its predicates.

Peter Brooks sees in the high-strung performance of melodrama its characteristic "excess" (*The Melodramatic Imagination* 5) which overwrites and overwhelms the text with its ineffable, unsayable unsaid. The body in melodrama is charged with meaning and acts out the recognition of the repressed: mute signs augment the inability to verbally acknowledge and say it all. Brooks's insight is validated in Ibsen's *Hedda Gabler*, in the eponymous heroine's acting out of an almost libidinal disgust. What unsettles Hedda most is her pregnancy, the text's biggest open secret. She internalizes the discursive norms of the dominant "classical" culture in her fear and loathing of heterogeneity, disproportion, symbolic gaps and filth—"I loathe all sorts of ugliness" (51). Hedda's statuesque, distinguished, and seemingly "opaque" (7) body, her "Ideal-Ich," also coincides with the body of becoming, the secreting, mutating flesh. The more she seeks to "kill time" (23), the more interminable it seems to get, and she is locked joylessly in the infinity of its bounded space. To her husband's adoration of her blooming figure she says "Oh, do be quiet—!" (9); again, when Tesman can barely hide his pleasure in the presence of Brack—"Doesn't she look flourishing? She has actually . . ."—Hedda begs to be left unnoticed (20); when Brack reminds her of the "stimulating experience" (32) she has in store, Hedda turns away in anger, refusing to actualize the possibility in language—"Be quiet! Nothing of that sort will ever happen!" (32). The only time she gets herself to articulate her expectancy, she is paralyzed in horror and ennui:

> HEDDA. Well, I may as well tell you that—just at this time—(*Impatiently, breaking off.*) No; no; you can ask Aunt Julia. She will tell you, fast enough . . . (*clenching her hands together in desperation*). Oh it is killing me,—it is killing me, all this! (63)

What the text cannot talk about is not Hedda's pregnancy, but that she sees it as a disorganization of her body. Her intense disavowal of the visceral symptomatically proclaims desire in the mode of denial: Hedda's inability to signify her desire, and designate its place or object, constitutes the void over which the play is constructed as a hypersign. If Lovborg is the tormented thinker and writer, the oedipal quest-hero, seeking a maternal object, Tesman his surrogate, and Thea the critic *manqué*, Hedda permeates the text as a negativity. As Elin Diamond states eloquently,

> her hysteria—her hysteron or womb—wanders into every corner of the play's perimeter, mimicking the discourse of her interlocutors—the language of womanly confidentiality with Thea; of wifely devotion with Tesman; of romantic dualism with Lovborg—infecting and destroying: "Why is it this—this curse—that everything I touch turns ridiculous and vile?" (75)

Repression and incipient hysteria make everything vile and absurd inevitably, not just in the sophisticated *Hedda Gabler,* but in the idyllic pastoral worlds evoked by Hazlewood's *Lady Audley's Secret* (1863) or Lewis's *The Bells* (1871). In Hazlewood's adaptation of Mary Elizabeth Braddon's popular novel, secrets refused to be consigned to subterranean depths quite literally, and catastrophically return to exact consequences. The most deadly in the lady's repertoire of mysteries, for her Royal Victoria audience anyway, is the possibility that, "We may have two faces" (241), as she darkly states in an aside. The details she tries to delete from her gentrified existence are a past marriage and the first husband, George Talboys. After consigning both to the bottom of a well, she has to also take care of the dastardly blackmailer who has witnessed the murder, and the increasingly suspicious Robert Audley, her nephew by marriage and the bereaved friend of Talboys. In consequence, she is visited by "abject fears and whisperings of conscience" (251), the death of Sir Audley, and later by the "murdered" set (who were never really "dead beyond doubt"), and madness. In *The Bells,* the village burgomaster experiences the horror of committing murder belatedly, when his past substantially returns to him in the sound of his victim's sleigh-bells and the sight of his victim's eyes. Referential displacements of the unsymbolizable or unsymbolized destroy Mathias's hard-earned familial and social stability. What Lacan calls the real, that part of reality that escapes symbolization, returns in the form of psychotic apparitions. Melodrama recoups itself by acting out the primordially repressed; the fictional world that seemed temporarily out of joint, imbricated in the protagonist's hysteria, ejects the traumatic element—that thing in it more than itself—out of its corpus. Lady Audley's dying words appropriately sublimate her purposeful withholding, her unmentionable secret, in the pity-tinged recrimination of her silent spectators: "Do not touch me—do not come near me—let me claim your silence—" (266).

Now, if, according to Brooks, melodramatic affect is a cumulative result of the inability, and consequent compulsion, to say everything, we can investigate, as Joan Copjec does, the nature of this inability. Is it one that issues from a prohibition, or the one that issues from impossibility? Copjec refers to Lacan's formulas of sexuation, the disparate solutions or compromise-formations resorted to by the sexes to deal with the impossibility of absolute satisfaction. The male child enters the socio-symbolic with tremendous loss on his pulse, with the sense of having given up something to get it all. For him totality can be had only when something has been excluded from it. For the female child however, castration is without the threat of prohibition, the father's interdiction, and precedes her entry into language. It is a different, non-phallic logic of sexual difference, one that constitutes subjectivity free of division. However, the girl's relation with the Other of society or language is also a failed one, not because it lacks something, but because everything can be included in it. If the universe of men is prohibited, that of women is impossible. If for man the word is death to the thing, for woman signification involves not a distancing from, but a presentification of an unlimited *jouissance*. As Copjec elucidates, "the imperative to include, or not say "no," does not give the woman any more opportunity to say everything than the imperative to exclude something, the parental interdiction, gives the man, since no all can form where inclusion knows no limit" (115). According to this reading, Brooks's theory of melodrama is informed by a masculine logic of lack and supplement, whereby a whole is simultaneously thought to exist and to require one more thing to complete itself. Copjec reads melodrama as a feminine relation to jouissance instead: the amplified affect of melodrama does not spring from a prohibition that closes off the diegetic space by excluding something from it, but is rather the cause of the diegesis's inability to close itself off. Melodrama is a "feminine" malady because no symbolic limit intervenes to inscribe its contingencies or authenticate its identity by eliminating inconsistencies. The logic of melodrama is an unbounded and non-identitarian one, or one that lies outside a phallic law of identification. The "more" of melodrama, Hedda's "wild dance on the piano," does not call the bluff on foreclosure, but actively displays the informalities of its diegetic reality and its lack of lack. While agreeing with and learning from most of Brooks's now very established perceptions of melodrama, I think Copjec's understanding of the melodramatic mode sheds light on its tremendous popularity in what Henry James characterized as "a feminine, nervous, hysterical, chattering, canting age" (Hadley 186). I will use her insights to make the claim that melodrama incarnates the central paradox of hysteria—affective disorder par excellence—where the hysteric has no body, and too much body. The hysterogenic body is a stand-in, a duplicitous simulacrum of the erotogenic body whose sexualization, and subsequent discursive formation, has somehow been truncated. The hysteric has no body because she could not symbolize the desiring physiological body. And the hysteric has too much body because the other body, the strange hysterogenic prosthesis, proclaims its will to pleasure in a circle of recapitulation and return. There is *both* the will to pleasure proclaimed by the body of *jouissance, and* the lack of a physical body through which to experience that pleasure. In the absence of the symbolic limits and laws of the body, the hysteric repudiates sexual difference and asks, from the place of her symptom: "Am I a man? Am I a woman? How are these identifications embodied? How are they signified? How do they determine a relation to the speaking subject?" (Kahane, *Passions of the Voice,* xi).

The symptom, where these contradictory and unbearable truths about the self are articulated and contested, should be seen as an "objective correlative" of self-awareness, not something that can be interpreted and thereby cured, but as what Lacan called "sinthome": "a stain correlative to the very (non)being of the subject" (*Tarrying with the Negative* 67). The signifying trace of melodrama strings along synecdochic parts that do not let us perceive totality because they are themselves failed wholes. There is no central character or preferred perspective, no guarantee, no solid ground from which the enunciation can take place. Instead of imitating a "daily reality," this kind of drama enacts a "dream reality."[2] *Eastenders* progressively unfolds over decades, showcasing events not necessarily teleological, an accretion of narrative fragments that cannot be constructed into an ontological whole, and an accumulation of people not convincingly related to each other or relevant to the plot. It is probably because melodrama is gripped with symbolic impotence, this inability to say it all, definitively and officially, that the imaginary limits it imposes seem all the more improbable and inauthentic. The traditional formulae, providential interventions, sensationalism, spectacular elaborations of meaning, objectification of virtue and vice, all bear testimony to the difficult task of imitating and aesthetically framing an unmanageable real. If the symbolic world seems eviscerated because it is too full, unfettered by limits, melodrama makes up for the lack that this world lacks by imposing contingent—all too contingent— boundaries. Joan Copjec identifies this as the ethical imperative of melodrama, whereby it fashions a hysterical rectification of its own symbolic failure by bringing vast powers of repression to bear on its own *jouissance.*

In 1819 Thomas John Dibdin publicized one of his dramatic pieces as "Melodrame Mad" (*Melodramatic Tactics* 1), placing the viewer in an analytical position or that of the superneurotic. In the world of melodrama, written or staged, we are invited to understand with our eyes, see with our heart, and cogitate with our nervous system. We listen for the symptom in mute gesture. We can even claim that our enjoyment of melodrama happens outside the symbolic, both in the sense that melodrama's inconsistencies make it unassimilable by signifiers and that it is a modality in which the symbolic itself comes up against its own inconsistencies. Looking at Victorian melodrama, what seems at first glance to be puerile and populist cultural reflexivity, soon defamiliarizes itself into a "Comic, Pathetic, Historic, Anachronasmatic, Ethic, Epic Melange" (Dibdin 1819), a veritable madwoman in culture's attic. Despite its shameless manipulation of plot to reinforce patriarchal values, its stock types and implausible denouements, nonsense blocks and diverts the series of sense in melodrama. A baroque construct of the symbolic, melodrama is also about the failure of the limits of the symbolic, the negation of no. A surplus of particulars trivializes and debunks universals in sympathetic exchanges of laughter and tears. Analysis is both necessary and interminable for the enigmas of melodrama: theory is possible only as impossible and unfinished for we do not know what we enjoy.

I. (MIS)RULE BRITANNIA

In Act III, Scene IV, of Douglas Jerrold's *Black-Ey'd Susan,* the play's naval hero William is seen beseeching his wife Susan to verbally articulate her farewell to him. "Now, what would you ask," he says, "have you nothing, nothing to say?"[3] Susan then speaks poignantly about her inability to speak, blaming it on an overloading of affect that will not let her pry open sign systems: "my heart swells to my throat, I can but look and weep" (41). It is hard not to attempt a taxonomic treatment of this scene, for it occurs almost generically in Victorian melodrama. In play after play, the heroine finds herself so subsumed in feeling, that a defection from *discours* seems inevitable and warranted in the theatrical code. While this effectively bolsters the visual dimension of melodrama, it also betrays strategies of representation that are situated on the borders of texts and contexts, aesthetics and ideology.

In his essay "Melodrama, Body, Revolution," Peter Brooks sees melodrama as valorizing what he calls "a certain semiotics of the body" (41). According to him, the melodramatic body is a body charged with meaning—melodrama disavows repression through hysteria, where what is played out in the symptom takes the place of a discourse that cannot be uttered. The melodramatic moment, says Brooks, "is a moment when the bodies behave nearly hysterically, if by hysteria we understand a condition of bodily writing, a condition in which the repressed affect is represented on the body" (21). The hysterical body, where psychic affect crystallizes into somatic effect, is also, typically, a feminized body. Peter Brooks sees the hysterical body in the tradition of Hippocrates and Freud, "as a woman's body, and indeed a victimized woman's body, on which desire has inscribed an impossible history, a story of desire in an impasse" (22). The signifying elaboration of desire takes shape through the symptom; the hysterized body is an expressionist apparatus, converting and codifying messages otherwise marginalized by the dominant logos. When we look at *Black-Ey'd Susan,* however, we find the male protagonist too in postures—or the bold imposture—of hysteria. Bodies, readable and interpretable like texts, populate the stage, and we are invited to read and interpret during the pauses in dramatic action, the freeze frames or tableaux that Martin Miesel calls "moment[s] of stasis" (52).

Till the end of 1828, the young Jerrold was a full-time and prolific writer of melodramas and farces for George Bowell Davidge, manager of the Coburg Theatre. This was the era of the monopoly of 'legitimate' drama by the patent or 'royal' theaters, Drury Lane, Covent Garden, and the Haymarket. The Licensing Act of 1737 allowed these theaters to stage conventional dramas with dialogue, while other 'minor' establishments were allowed song and dance, mime and burletta. The spectacle and song that were originally interspersed with dialogue to circumvent the ban soon cultivated a rambunctious theatrical taste that favored farce, burlesque, melodrama, and extravaganza. Douglas Jerrold had supplied the Coburg Theatre plays like *The Living Skeleton* (1825), *Popular Felons* (1826), *The Tower of Lochlain, or the Idiot Son* (1828), *Fifteen Years of a Drunkard's Life* (1828), when the actor-manager Robert Elliston managed to lure him away to the Surrey Theatre, a major London 'minor.' [4] Minor theaters were vortices of the peculiar cultural elements of the communities in which they were situated: "they were London theatres and provincial theatres at the same time" (Slater 16). As William Hazlitt reported in his article in *The London Magazine* (March 1920), the drama critic went to these smaller theatres "not only willing, but determined to be pleased. We had laid aside the pedantry of rules, the petulance of sarcasm, and had hoped to open once more, by stealth, the source of sacred tears, of bubbling laughter, and concealed sighs. We were not formidable. On the contrary, we were made of penetrable stuff"(Rowell 178). *Black Ey'd Susan* flourished in the interpersonal and decentralized structure of a Minor. Opening at Surrey on June 8, 1829, it clocked up 150 consecutive nights at the Surrey, 400 performances in 1829 at different London theaters, and many more at provincial ones. T. P. Cooke, to whose "perfect acting" Jerrold attributed "the prosperity of the production" (Knight 59), performed the role of William over 800 times. Cooke, with his mastery of the double hornpipe, was a sure box-office hit in sensational dramas exalting sailors; though a sailor himself, "this does not appear to have inhibited him in his many impersonations of stage seamen" as Michael Booth wryly comments on the actor's method (*The Revels History of Drama in English VI* 218). The play skillfully trapped claps, drew laughter and tears of sympathy. So strong was the emotional valence of William's farewell to his wife in III. iv, that it was used by W. G. Wills in 1873, in a rather different context: as a model for the king's farewell speech in *Charles the First*.

"Melodramas directed at the naïve grow numerous in this decade," observes Booth in his review of dramatic activity between 1820 and 1830 (*Revels History VI*); true to its kind, *Black-Ey'd Susan* abounds in stereotypes, attempted murders, near seductions, hidden secrets, purloined posts. Susan is separated from her husband, William, through the machinations of her wicked uncle and landlord Doggrass who forced him to turn sailor, and seeks to turn her homeless. Gothic meets domestic in Doggrass, who could be seen as a version of the incestuous father-figure in that he orchestrates the scene of Susan's attempted seduction. He is in league with the dubious Hatchet, who concocts the story of William's death in order to marry Susan, and tries to facilitate this alliance in order to strengthen his association with the group of smugglers. William's fleet docks as Susan is beset by the amorous advances of the smuggler. But just when he has shielded his wife from the greed, lechery, and subterfuge of the locals and is "as merry as a ship's crew on a pay day" (36), his superior officer, Captain Crosstree, lustfully, and in a drunken state, accosts Susan. William, not knowing who the man is that he sees attacking Susan, rushes up and strikes him. He is court-martialed consequently for striking a superior officer, and is about to die, when he is saved by a timely reprieve, and in the final recognition scene, virtue triumphs while Doggrass goes down "with the horror of the good and the laughter of the wicked weighing on his drowning head" (p. 38). The captain makes a dramatic entrance just as the noose is about to be tightened around William's neck, flaunting a document that officially releases William from the king's service. William had appealed for a discharge earlier, and it had been granted to him, and though the inveigling Doggrass attempts to avoid the disclosure of the document, it is finally revealed that William was not a sailor when he struck his officer. The Captain redeems himself to become a poster-child for temperance. Lieutenant Pike and his troop of marines arrest the smugglers. Doggrass' malice is overcome by his own maladroitness; on his way to hear the court-martial proceedings, he grows so eager to hear William's death warrant that he slips overboard a small boat and drowns.

The stupendous successes of the British Navy during the period of the French Revolution and the Napoleonic Wars (1792–1815) associated the nautical character with public, patriotic masculinity—melodramas like *Black-Ey'd Susan* evolved from nautical spectacle dramas like *The Siege, Storming, and Taking of Badajoz* and *The Siege of Salamanca,* both performed in 1812, *The Siege of Gibralter* (1804), *The Battle of Trafalgar* (1806), *The Battle of the Nile* (1815), and *The Battle of Waterloo* (1824) which celebrated the age of Wellington, Nelson, the Peninsular Army, and the glorious fleet, and whose engagements were spectacularly fought at Sadler's Wells and Astley's circus ring.[5] The audiences were almost entirely working and lower middle class: watermen, shipbuilders, seamen, chandlers, dockworkers, and their womenfolk, their lives revolving around the Thames and the sea, their livelihoods linked to Britain's maritime prowess. Jack Gallant, Jack Stedfast, Bill Bluff, Union Jack, Ben Billows—all characters played with aplomb by T. P. Cooke—fought wreckers, pirates, smugglers, ruminated on their officers, their ships, and their country in an unnatural sea-metaphor, and were also domestic creatures, promoting family values and life on shore. The appeal of *Black-Ey'd Susan*—which remained the most popular melodrama of the century—lay in a clever superimposition of domestic verisimilitudes on socio-political ones. Occurring, as Jeffrey Cox notes, "a full decade after the challenges of the revolutionary and Napoleonic years were past," *Black-Ey'd Susan* presents the sailor as a defender of status quo, "purging naval history of its radical elements and transfer[ring] the cultural authority of past British naval victories onto a vision of the domestic order in the present" (173). Sweet William is also the all too human face of the nautical persona. Jerrold reworks the reactionary potential of the Napoleonic sailor type to show instead how William is forced to become a sailor by economic necessity, the plight of the poor on land, and the kind of economical tyranny represented by Doggrass. Jerrold's stage tar in *Black Ey'd Susan* romanticizes alike the conditions of being at home and at sea. William curiously valorizes familial pleasures in the very language of normative masculinity that estranges him from them. To quote Cox again, he, "like the Gothic or romantic figure, has left behind the confines of his home and yet, unlike these troubling presences, desires only to return to his home and all it represents" (178).

William, according to the testimony of his crew, is

> The trimmest sailor as ever handled rope; the first on his watch, the last to leave the deck; one as never belonged to the after-guard—he has the cleanest top, and the whitest hammock; from reefing a main

top-sail to stowing a netting, give me taut Bill afore any able seaman
in his Majesty's fleet. (35)

His self-division—his "double-conscience" which Freud and Breuer, later in
the century would call the "hypnoid state" and identify as the predominant
hysterical symptom—follows the familiar psychic topography of a strictly
differentiated, and antagonistic inside and outside. Testimony at the trial
summarizes the contradictions in duty forced on the sailor, for "William cut
down his [superior] officer in defense of his wife" (31). William exculpates
himself on the ground of his inevitable self-estrangement: "all I wish, whilst
you pass sentence, is your pity. That your honours, whilst it is your duty to
condemn the sailor, may, as having wives you honour and children you love,
respect the husband" (37). He seems to alienate, rather than identify with
his nautical persona as he performs it with the metonymic excess of mimicry.
Like Ploughshare, the farmer, whom William interrogates anxiously about
Susan upon his arrival, we feel the lack of an overtly meaningful content in
William's speech quite acutely:

> *William.* Avast there! if you must hoist the black flag—gently. Is she yet
> in commission?—Does she live?
>
> *Ploughshare.* She does.
>
> *William.* Thank heaven! . . . but your figurehead changes like a dying
> dolphin; she lives, but perhaps hove down in the port of sickness. No!
> what then, eh—avast! Not dead—not sick—yet—why there's a galley
> fire lighted up in my heart—there's not an R put in her name?
>
> *Ploughshare.* What do you mean?
>
> *William.* Mean! Grape and canister! She's not run—not shown false
> colours?
>
> *Ploughshare.* No, no. (20)

The interpretable discontinuity marks precisely the gap between bodies and
the texts they impersonate, which is also a space of enjoyment. The play
seems to suggest that William is always already hysterized—"for the gilt
swabs on the shoulders can't alter the heart that swells beneath" (36)—his
public and private priorities are mutually canceling and his relation to his
reference truly aberrant. *Black-ey'd Susan* gives play to what Peter Stallybrass
and Allon White call "the inmixing of the subject, to the heterodox, messy,
excessive and unfinished formalities of the body and social life" (182–183).

William projects a totality of image as well as a lack—the peripatetic sailor, at home everywhere and nowhere, both an image of man, and a composite of images.

"We go not so much to hear as to look," said Percy Fitzgerald in 1870 in his *Principles of Comedy and Dramatic Effect,* and we can extend his insight from its immediate context to critically assess the spectacular affect of Jerrold's play. "It is like a giant peep-show, and we pay the show-man, and put our eyes to the glass and stare" (30). The female protagonist of *Black-Ey'd Susan* is, predictably, the primary object of voyeurism, and of a desire that metonymically proliferates to generate the diegetic text. She is "that pretty piece of soft-speaking womanhood" (5); single-minded and unreflecting, she is indistinguishable from the contingencies of her situa-tion as the wife of the "jovial sailor" (6) William; she is the "prettiest little vessel" (20) and William lovingly refers to her as "my craft" (19), and "the petticoat" (22); a cipher in the nautical rhetoric of the play; she is also the substance of a song. In her representation is dramatized the dilemma of anthropomorphizing what is traditionally thought of as unrepresentable, woman being, in the word's of Hatchet, "like sealing wax" easily malleable to given forms, and readily available for tropological manipulation. She is referred to as a value-object: Hatchet threatens to "buy" her heart "with the chink" (15); Gnatbrain fantasizes about being her landlord, accepting song in lieu of money (9); she is compared to tokens of Imperialist traffic, diamonds, spice, and ivory (26); and she is the collateral—"a sailor's own sheet-anchor"(34)—for which William unwittingly risks his naval career. But, if tokens are also signs, and signs that speak, Susan is from the start doomed to asymbolia. Her "to-be-looked-at-ness" (to borrow a term from Laura Mulvey) constitutes her as a blindspot in the play, which in turn pri-oritizes William as the possessor of the gaze, and eroticizes the spectacle of the spectator. Susan performs the *objet a* function, radically contentless, and the absent cause of a metonymically proliferating desire. William's fantasy is an elaborate artifice that cloaks her non-existence:

> I have been three years at sea; all the time I have heard but once from Susan—she has been to me a main-stay in all weathers. I have been piped up—roused from my hammock, dreaming of her—for the cold black middle watch; I have walked the deck, the surf beating in my face, but Susan was at my side, and I did not feel it; I have been reefing on the yards, in cold and darkness, when I could hardly see the hand of my next messmate—but Susan's eyes were on me, and there was light. (19–20)

What William senses is the object as an absence, a projected fantasy. He enters the stage in a tumult of emotions—the narrating "I" of these passages, the eye through which the reader witnesses, emerges as the eye seeing itself, ultimately reducing the reader to an effect of its narcissistic voyeurism:

> *William.* Huzza, huzza! my noble fellows, my heart jumps like a dolphin—my head turns around like a capstern; I feel as if I were driving before the gale of pleasure for the haven of joy. (18)

In the spirals of power and avowable pleasure that turns it, and which it turns, the subject hysterically splits in enunciation, and views itself as an object:

> *William.* What! and am I left alone in the doctor's list, whilst all the crew are engaging? I know I look as lubberly as a Chinese junk under a jewry mast. I'm afraid to throw out a signal—my heart knocks against my timbers, like a jolly boat in a breeze, alongside a seventy-four. Damn it, I feel as if half of me was wintering in the Baltic, and the other half stationed in Jamaica. (19)

Hysteria at once stages the gaze at the self, and imposes limits on it, bars it, declares it not-all. Despite being the locus of the excessive verbal energy of the play, William occasionally shares his wife's inability to speak. William's "nautical" speech, seemingly immured in socially created meaning, is disrupted by the pulsional, semiotic pressures. In Scene 1 of Act II, for instance, it loses fixity of signification in an emotional impasse:

> When land was cried from the mast head, I seized the glass—my shipmates saw the cliffs of England—I, I could see but Susan! I leap upon the beach; my shipmates find hands to grasp and lips to press—I find not Susan's. (20)

His words are overcome by the ardency of the unspoken. As Peter Brooks says of mute gesture, his speech is "a sign *for* a sign" (*The Melodramatic Imagination* 72), metaphorical insofar as it tries to grant immanence to a grandiose, yet ineffable emotional integer. When the nautical inflection is at its strongest, the metaphorics of William's speech gives it an almost physical immediacy, giving meaning a distinctly bodily character (the speech and the body of the sailor becoming interchangeable ciphers). In Scene I of Act II, William tries to regain composure after hearing Susan's name:

> William: Avast there! hang it—that name, spoke by another, has brought
> the salt water up; I can feel one tear standing in either eye like a marine
> at each gangway: but come, let's send them below. (19)

The act of shedding tears, unmanly as it is, delectably denies repression. At the same time, the nautical verbiage tries to contain overwhelming affect by conferring on it sign-status ("one tear . . . like a marine"). That which is unsignifiable in language, is nevertheless seen transversally through an overdetermined, value-coded sign system. "I should like," William says, "to beat all my feelings to quarters, that they may stand will to their guns, in this their last engagement": and yet, he laments, "My heart is splitting" (41). The strictly symbolic is swamped by another discourse, in which the cogito speaks inaudibly from the real of the body.

The negotiation William attempts between his "female malady" and normative masculinity makes for what Barbara Gelpi has called "the politics of androgyny."[6] If William's speech becomes psychosomatic, like the hysterical "talking body," it serves a double purpose. It constitutes a false universal whereby William traverses both male and female positions, and makes for a curious passive-aggressive performance, not unlike that of the hysterics in Charcot's medical theater in the Salpêtrière. The French neurologist Jean-Martin Charcot staged the pantomime of symptoms during the 1870s and 1880s where female hysterics under hypnosis "acted out their identifications, adopting poses, reliving roles, and re-enacting the past as they embodied a pre-existing and unconscious script before the eyes of a male spectator who, as in the theater of the time, was an essential part of the performance" (Robinson 17). William too, animated by the spectatorial gaze, enacts a curious entanglement of mastery and loss—mastery of voice necessarily wrested from and punctuated by immobilizing silences. In the trial scene he interrupts effusive accounts of himself by his shipmates, and, unlike Susan, manages to steal a look at his own looked-at-ness: "Your honours, I feel as if I were in irons, or seized to the grating, to stand here and listen—like the landlord's daughter of the Nelson—to nothing but yarns about service and character" (36). Again, after his death sentence,

> ADMIRAL *and* CAPTAINS *come forward*—ADMIRAL *shakes hands*
> *with* WILLIAM *who, overcome, kneels—after a momentary struggle, he*
> *rises, collects himself, and is escorted from the cabin in the same way that he*
> *entered.* (37)

William's hysteria also facilitates the co-optation of a multivalent hysterical imago, which, however problematic, widened behavioral options for Victorian ladies. The audience of Victorian melodrama has its cake and eats it too. The male-identified viewers can be enticed by hysterical "females" without being threatened by them—like the captain and the admiral in William's judgment scene, "men who had looked upon shipwreck, wounds and death with dry eyes," they can even cry, "when the business was over, like soft-hearted girls" (38). Through the transferential circuits of hysteria they can, in fact, indulge in the disorders and excesses of "femininity," inhabiting it as it were, yet secure in the recognition that it is also a formula, a cheap trick, a purchasable ticket.

Not surprisingly, the play's resolution requires William's disenfranchisement from the king's navy; as the timely intervention of Captain Crosstree reveals, when William struck him he was a discharged sailor, therefore unimpeachable under the "twenty-second Article of War" (37) which imposes the death penalty on any man in the Fleet who lifts his hand against his superior officer. William the sailor turns out not to be a sailor after all—he will henceforth stay on land, may be even with "six feet square for the cultivation of potatoes" (29). It is my contention that William's defection from *discours,* though manipulated aesthetically for laughs, is retroactively constructed as a culpable offense. He is not redeemed in the end for pitting morality and sentimentality against a heroic ideal, but readily discharged from service. What Brooks calls the "melodramatic imagination" is also historically specific, and in the nineteenth century it was characterized by high carnivalesque spirits *and* conservative ends. Victorian melodrama was one of "active participants in the discursive contests that resulted in that era's productions of meaning" (Hadley 7), social, cultural, and political. Male hysteria on the Victorian stage focalized specific moments of crisis, when discrepancies between a substantive category and its performance could be enjoyed surreptitiously before their subsequent delegitimation. The hysterical body—often seen interchangeably as the actor's body—replicated social identity without being reduced by it, making visible, through parodic repetition, the operation of self-replication in discourse. The aesthetic hysteric of melodrama functioned as a truly chiasmic figure, signifying the professionalization of play, as well as the playfulness, histrionic potential, and insincerity of 'honest' work. The spectating public of nautical melodramas granted tremulous assent to the spectacularized dissemination of a cherished ideal, as if to wish it away, and wish for "real people" who would continue to rule the waves on their behalf.

II. "IS THAT A MADWOMAN?"

Later that century, Archer in the *World* of 1896 reviewed *Black Ey'd Susan* as a "dear old piece of nautical nonsense." Plot and characterization in melodrama had indeed changed enough by then for Sweet William to be treated as a curiosity, a theatrical dinosaur, "a degenerate Briton, an unworthy compatriot of Nelson and Captain Marryat, who refuses to laugh at the first act, and to feel in the second act" (357). By Saturday, 27 May 1893, when *The Second Mrs Tanqueray* opened at St. James, melodrama had come of age and had new names. "This is a play for grown-up people" wrote Arthur Wing Pinero to Edmund Gosse, welcoming one of the cognoscenti invited to the first night of his *The Second Mrs Tanqueray* (Dawick 191). Though grounded still in the occasional opacity of mute, material signifiers, melodrama could now translate and articulate a tremendous range of mental states. To its arsenal of pictorial effects it added psychological ones, and instead of a series of highly charged situations, there was systematic narrativization. In place of desemanticized hysterical bodies in the arrest of tableau, we now had a linguistic corpus, which seemed to generate the malaise, and deflect every appeal for adequation, response, or recognition. We are left dicing with uncertainty paradoxically because the text is in overdrive to leave nothing unexplained, and is relentless in its almost novelistic effort to match effect with etiology, and make everything obvious.

In paranoid anticipation of the corrupting influence of Pinero's play, T. W. M. Lund, Chaplain of the Chapel of the blessed Virgin Mary, Liverpool, published a tract entitled " 'The Second Mrs. Tanqueray;' What? and Why?" in the spirit of clarifying "momentous points of morality very likely to be misunderstood" (3), which rapidly sold out nine editions. He sets up his argument around two rhetorical questions: "Who is 'Mrs. Tanqueray'?" and "Who is responsible for her?" The answer to the first is simply that she is "a type of a class, rather than an individual" (5). The second question is duly addressed with the unhesitating conviction that the person responsible for the woman's fate is she herself. Lund writes with millennial misgiving that in these transitional times, women "of whose goodness I have no question" are traipsing on a borderland, "of the perils of which they are quite ignorant" (15), teetering on the brink of a vertiginous fall. He sees Paula as a type of a floating signifier, an abnormal appetite glutting on a rapid sequence of sensations, a plurality of beguiling images: "Loose familiarity, laxity of language, risky allusions, the air of knowing too much, mannish ways, unwomanly liberties, all this is not to make for women's advancement, but to fill sane people with apprehension" (15–16). The cure, if any, for this crisis of morals is in the hands of men, and their self-respect and self-control. Lund ends his sermon with a call to his fellow men to pity and protect the weaker sex while also cultivating reverence for woman as woman, not without invoking a stirring image of women who are already wreckage, "the jetsam and flotsam of the social sea" (21). Legitimizing the Reverend's concern, and attaching a pecuniary value to its moral one, is an advertisement on the back of the tract for a "SCHOOL FOR LADIES, UNDER THE DIRECTION OF REV. T. W. M. LUND, M. A. CAMB., AND MRS LUND, ASSISTED BY A STAFF OF FIRST-CLASS ENGLISH AND FOREIGN TEACHERS."

The principle actor of the play, which, as one "old school" critic described in the *Times* as holding the spectator from first to last "in the thrall of a horrible fascination,"[7] is Paula, a young woman who has been the mistress of several rich playboys, and who marries into the gentrified world of Aubrey Tanqueray, a middle-aged widower. Aubrey foresees this unequal alliance as potentially destructive of his social status, but commits to it anyway, considering the unhappiness of his first marriage and the decision of his only child, Ellean, to take monastic orders. The play begins in Aubrey's bachelor flat in London, where he ceremoniously bids farewell to assiduously cultivated homosocial bonds with his closest friends, Frank Misquith, Gordon Jayne, and Cayley Drummle. As he says ominously, "in nine cases out of ten a man's marriage severs for him more close ties than it forms" (SMT 145). Cayley Drummle, who joins the party a little after Aubrey's dismal and mystifying pronouncements, inadvertently lays down the definition of a "horrible *mesalliance*" (SMT 146) and elaborates its consequences. He cites the instance of George Orreyed who has committed himself to social obsolescence by marrying Mabel Hervey, "a lady who would have been, perhaps has been, described in the reports of the police or the Divorce Court as an actress" (SMT 147). Drummle typifies late-Victorian attitudes when he invokes the curious non-presence of an actress:

> Physically, by the strange caprice of creation, beautiful; mentally, she lacks even the strength of deliberate viciousness. Paint her portrait, it would symbolise a creature perfectly patrician; lance a vein of her superbly modelled arm, you would get the poorest *vin ordinaire!* Her affections, emotions, impulses, her very existence—a burlesque! Flaxen, five-and-twenty, and feebly frolicsome; anybody's, in less gentle society I should say everybody's, property! (147)

Paula too is a woman who was once "everybody's property," and her attempts to move away and upward, from a masculinist society's traffic in low-class women to a respectable subset, occasion severe apprehension and lampooning. Drummle emphasizes the notion of an iteratively constructed, burlesque-like identity when he heaps a barrage of names on Paula: "Mrs-Miss Jarman-Mrs Ray-Miss Ray" (155). The iconography of the fallen woman precedes Paula, and an alienating objectification has already begun. Drummle muses on her imago with the ambivalence of a Freud staring at Medusa's Head, petrified at the sight of a multiplicity that beguilingly sheaths castrating lack.

Not surprising for someone consigned from the outset to the "social Dead Sea" (148), Paula exudes a diapason of emotions in her first appearance: seemingly lighthearted, she mentions thoughts of suicide at the event of being rejected yet again.

> Paula: Do you know, I feel certain I should make away with myself if anything serious happened to me.
>
> Aubrey: Anything serious! What, has nothing ever been serious to you, Paula?
>
> Paula: Not lately; not since a long while ago. I made up my mind then to have done with taking things seriously. If I hadn't, I—However, we won't talk about that. (156–60)

She has started uncharacteristically to live in earnest, and will soon die of it.

Just as Paula proclaims her satisfaction with the state of things, there is a reflux of discontentment in her life in the form of Ellean, who eschews convent life to rejoin her father. Act Two embroils her in a spiral of ennui, desperation, and envy. Paula misses city life ("London or Heaven! Which is farther from me!" 162), is irked by Aubrey's growing sanctimoniousness and also his idealization of Ellean, and stung by Ellean's and the neighbors' systematic rejection of her. She fixates on Ellean and her desire for her approval grows proportionately to Ellean's utter non-regard. Aubrey calls it a "feverish, jealous attachment" (168). Paula puts forth a rationale of sorts for coveting this friendship:

> PAULA: I'm sure Aubrey, that the love of a nice woman who believed me to be like herself would do me a world of good. You'd get the benefit of it as well as I. It would soothe me; it would make me less horribly restless; it would take this—this—mischievous feeling from me. (165)

She herself deploys psychological talk to get at the recalcitrant Ellean. Poking fun at Ellean's belief that her dead mother has an afterlife in her dreams, and guides her through them, Paula states brutally that "Dreams are only a hash-up of one's day-thoughts. . . . if you cared for me in the daytime I should soon make friends with those nightmares of yours" (167). She then confesses to painful memories that she has repressed for long, and asks Ellean to help her confront them.

PAULA: A few years ago I went through some trouble, and since then I haven't shed a tear. I believe if you put my arms round me just once I should run upstairs and have a good cry. There, I've talked to you as I've never talked to a woman in my life. Ellean, you seem to fear me. Don't! Kiss me! (167)

Ellean shrinks from her, as though fearing a venereal contamination, and the session plunges Paula in deeper despair.

It is around this time that Cayley Drummle reenters the dramatic scene. He is the Tiresias-like lynchpin of the social set he so magisterially oversees. He is a reporter of gossip, an arbiter of proprieties, the third party in transactions, who also keeps watchful sentry on the shores of the social Dead Sea, waiting "For some of my best friends *to come up*" (148). Early in the play he reminds Aubrey of his spectatorial license, and the "old-fashioned" playgoer's contract with the bodies on stage: like him or her, Drummle is after aesthetic gratification from seeing "certain characters happy and comfortable at the finish" (156). His statement, "I *live* in the world" (155) is both a constative and performative speech-act, to whose authority Paula and Aubrey pay homage by making him the custodian of their confidences. It is with Drummle that Aubrey discusses the symptomatology of Paula's disorder. Aubrey sees Paula's past as having "maimed" (169) her, rendering her incapable of bourgeois discretion. Not only are her ideas improper and strange, she seems to have no reservations about disseminating them: "her words, acts even, have almost lost their proper significance for her, and seem beyond her control" (169). To Aubrey's anxiety that this kind of information might damage the virginal Ellean psychologically, Drummle recommends worldly knowledge for Ellean, and the sounder, more philosophical judgment that results from it, over an impossible and absurd innocence. He even arranges for Ellean to go abroad (Paris no less) with Mrs Cortelyon, who is willing to suppress her misgivings about Paula and reestablish contact with the Tanquerays. Paula reacts to this new development and to Ellean's spontaneous acceptance of her neighbor with asperity and insolence first, and then in paroxysms of rage and despair.

ELLEAN I should like to go with Mrs Cortelyon—

PAULA Ah!

ELLEAN that is, if—if—

PAULA If—if what?

ELLEAN (looking towards *Aubrey, appealingly*) Papa?

PAULA (*in a hard voice*) Oh, of course—I forgot. (*To Aubrey*) My dear
Aubrey, it rests with you, naturally, whether I am—to lose—Ellean.
(174–75)

"Is that a madwoman?" (175) wonders Mrs Cortelyon at Paula's fury, raw at
times, and sublimated in the rites of formal social exchange at others. Paula's
past extradiegetically shapes the plot through traumatic flashback: "I have
never felt like this—except once—in my life" (175). As if to confront it more
fully, Paula goes back to associates of her order, and invites the obnoxious
Orreyeds to Highercoombe.

Sir George and Lady Orreyed, "Dodo" and "Birdie" to each other, provide comic respite in the ensuing scenes of Paula's growing emotional incon-
tinence. Paula is increasingly restless, consumed by her distaste for the antics
of the Orreyeds, and despair at the state of her marriage. She risks an even
greater estrangement from her own sense of self when she jealously intercepts
Ellean's letters to Aubrey. Drummle urges her to come clean, and then, holds
a mirror to her sleep-deprived face. This is a momentous gesture, freezing
as it does the instant when the gazing subject locks eyes with the gazed-at
object. Paula returns to the corporeal site of her crime and punishment in
a fatal short-circuiting of the externally determined gaze and her internally
motivated self-gaze. "You brute, Cayley, to show me that!" she exclaims, adding "You'll kill me, amongst you!" (184).

What is even worse, Aubrey now excavates, seemingly on behalf of
Paula, an unreachably anterior self, when Paula was "like Ellean":

You hadn't a thought that wasn't a wholesome one, you hadn't an
impulse that didn't tend towards good, you never harboured a notion
you couldn't have gossiped about to a parcel of children. (186)

As Aubrey Tanqueray demonstrates, it is the absence of limit in the hysteric's world, the lack of prohibition that ordinarily structures symbolic reality,
which makes her unsanctioned enjoyment so unbearable:

You're not mistress any longer of your thoughts or your tongue. Why,
how often, sitting between you and Ellean, have I seen her cheeks turn
scarlet as you've rattled off some tale that belongs by right to the club or
the smoking room! Have you noticed the blush? (186)

Ellean returns from her travels with a blush of a different kind, and
with Hugh Ardale, an army officer who has won Ellean's love with accounts

of his bravery in colonial contexts. Ellean finally turns towards Paula in yet another departure from her saintliness, and Paula comes face to face with Hugh. In this close encounter with her past, we are given a glimpse into the pathogenesis of hysteria, and traumas that, however latent and dematerialized, always return:

> PAULA Oh! Oh! What happened to that flat of ours in Ethelbert Street?
>
> HUGH I let it.
>
> PAULA All that pretty furniture?
>
> HUGH Sold it.
>
> PAULA I came across the key of the escritoire the other day in an old purse! (*Suddenly realizing the horror and hopelessness of her position, and starting to her feet with an hysterical cry of rage*) What am I maundering about? (195)

The non-referential maundering results from the traumatic impasse between the desire to express sexuality and a resistance against it. As if to escape the symbolic containment of *jouissance* Paula depopulates different roles, emptying them of solidity in a ghastly chain of reiterated disillusions. "This will send me mad!" (195) she says. Hugh, rattled at the thought of losing Ellean, a woman "as good as my own mother" (196), threatens and begs an unyielding Paula to keep her silence. The third act ends and the next begins with intransitive, picturesque moments—Paula staring at her own reflection in a little silver mirror—reminders of the immanence of a panoptic vision that turns Paula's body into a simulacrum of itself.

In the last act, Ellean masters ineffable integers to construct a case history of Paula. They lock eyes first in a highly specular moment:

> PAULA But, Ellean, you forget I—I am your stepmother. It was my— my duty—to tell your father what I—what I knew—
>
> ELLEAN What you knew! Why, after all, what can you know! You can only speak from gossip, report, hearsay! How is it possible that you—!
>
> *She stops abruptly. The two women stand staring at each other for a moment; then Ellean backs away from Paula slowly.*
>
> Paula!

PAULA What—what's the matter?

ELLEAN You—you knew Captain Ardale in London! (206)

Ellean declares that she has always known what Paula is. Not from gossip, report, or hearsay, but from the irrepressible body language of the fallen woman: "From the first moment I saw you I knew you were altogether unlike the good women I'd left" (207). The secret etiology of her hysterical disposition is suddenly transliterated by material signifiers ("It—it's in my face" says Paula in horror, 207). For all the shambolic inconsistencies in her behavior, all the hysterical highs and lows she emplots, the sentence passed on her in this judgment scene is unequivocal. Ellean's rhetoric brings to mind another detection scene, in *Lady Audley's Secret,* when Robert Audley relishes Lady Audley's increasing discomfiture under scrutiny:

> *Lady Audley.* . . . Are you fond of flowers, Mr. Audley?
>
> *Robert.* Very, but the flower I most value you do not seem to possess.
>
> Lady Audley. And that is—
>
> Robert. Heart's-ease!
>
> Lady Audley [aside]. What does he mean? [Aloud.] Heart's-ease? Well, you see, Mr. Audley, I have so much of my own that I can afford to dispense with its botanical name-sake.
>
> Robert. Indeed! I have remarked lately that you have been very ill at ease.
>
> Lady Audley. How kind of you to watch my health closely. I fancied I was looking remarkably well.
>
> *Robert.* You *appear* so, but you are not; your eyes are not half so bright as they were when I first came here. . . . Your manner is more anxious—you fall into deep reflection, and sometimes do not answer until you have been twice spoken to, then you suddenly rally and assume a levity which is forced and unnatural in my eyes. (*Nineteenth-Century Plays,* 253–54)

This melodramatic character vivisection also invokes the Contagious Diseases Acts of 1864, 1866, and 1869; military reforms which sought to prevent the spread of venereal disease among soldiers and sailors. Under these acts, plainclothes policemen were empowered to "detect" prostitutes among the women in the streets, presumably with the righteous rage of Ellean and Robert. The women were then coerced into a physical examination conducted by an autho-rized physician, and confined up to three months in "lock hospitals" if found diseased. The theatrical irony of Pinero's play lies in the fact that in this very specular moment between the two women, Ellean's act of "recognition" is, to Paula, one of grave misrecognition. It is a non-encounter with a resistant other that fills Paula with anxiety: to see without one's own gaze being returned is to recede into the nonmeaning of one's identity, and to experience one's own extinction as subject: "Ellean, I'm a good woman! I swear I am! I've always been a good woman! You dare to say I've ever been anything else! It's a lie!" (207). As Paula contemplates the traumatic void that underlies her fits and fantasies, Aubrey still espouses change, and talks of a future. "I believe the future is only the past again, entered through another gate" (209), declares Paula with finality. To the proliferation of ideas and images that her presence evokes in the play, Paula adds one last vision of a projected future:

> You'll see me then, at last, with other people's eyes. . . . A worn-out crea-ture—broken up, very likely, some time before I ought to be—my hair bright, my eyes dull, my body too thin or too stout, my cheeks raddled and ruddled—a ghost, a wreck, a caricature, a candle that gutters, call such an end what you like! (211)

Emphasizing the "hypnoid" structure of Pinero's play, where opposed char-acters grandiosely enact bipolar propensities *within* individual psyches, Elin Diamond points out how, "Her body in full view, Paula speaks of a body not present: a referent which, in the play's "double conscience," is more real than the one we see" (73). The intimate becomes extimate as Paula's desire is finally transmogrified into a narcissistic, highly eroticized, death drive.[8] As Lacan might have put it, the phallus appears in the social field, no longer merely supposed by the Oedipal structure. We glimpse at a horror-tinged *jouissance,* a place far beyond the pleasure principle, shuddering in parox-ysmal pain. Bataille described this enjoyment best as "a desire to die, but at the same time a desire to live with ever-greater intensity at the borderline between possible and impossible. It is a desire to live whilst ceasing to live, or to die without ceasing to live" (*L'Erotisme* 262). Paula exits (through the win-dow) soon after, and finally manages to get the attention and forgiveness she coveted from Ellean: "I heard the fall. I—I've seen her. . . . If I had only been merciful!" (211–12). Her departure marks the fissure in the diegetic reality through which the next hysteric, or the next hysterical sequence, can pervade it. Ellean is now seen enacting Paula's disorder: beating her breast, she mut-ters "But I know—I helped to kill her," as Cayley Drummle "*stands looking out*" (212) of the drawing room, or the 'lock' hospital. His speechlessness marks another neurotic breakdown, a catastrophic point at which the social text fails to assume a minimal distance from the phantasmatic.

The Second Mrs Tanqueray opened to great critical euphoria and disquiet, best captured in William Archer's 31st May review in the *Theatrical 'World'* for 1893. Archer praises Pinero's play as "virile" as opposed to "childish" art, a fine thing worth doing, that signaled the playwright's emancipation from box-office returns and booking-sheets:

> If I had the wit, I should like to write such a preface to *Mrs Tanqueray* as Dumas is in the habit of prefixing to his own plays, not criticising, in the narrow sense of the word, but explaining and expanding them. The limitations of *Mrs Tanqueray* are really the limitations of the dramatic form. (130)

Archer goes on to describe the curious non-pleasurable aesthetics of the play:

> Frankly it is not a play I hanker after seeing again. I want to read it, to study it—but, with Mrs Patrick Campbell in the title part, though, or because, her performance is almost perfect in its realism, the sensation it gave one could not at any point be described as pleasure. It interests and absorbs on; it satisfies the intelligence more completely than any other modern English play; but it is not in the least moving. Not once during the whole evening were the tears anywhere near my eyes. (131–132)

In his essay, "Pineroticism and the problem play," Joel H. Kaplan analyses the role of Mrs Patrick Campbell, who, with her performance of the title role had mobilized the authorial efforts to entertain as well as disturb his audience. To Paula's ferocity and restlessness, Mrs Pat brought an intensified restraint, suggestive of a past gentility that Pinero had not specified in his text. Her etiolated body—presaging a sensibility that was "Beardsleyesque, Baudelairean, and 'fin-de-sickly'"[9]—and her "Channel Steamer" voice both conveyed nausea and despair. She outlined her theatrical style years later in instructing John Gielgud, Oswald to her Mrs Alving in *Ghosts:* "Keep still, gaze at me. Empty your voice of meaning and speak as if you are going to be sick. Pinero told me this, I have never forgotten it" (Dent 286). Her "anorexic eroticism," as Kaplan describes it (47), suggested a beauty which was predatory of male vitality—as reflected in the iconography of Philip Burne-Jones's painting "The Vampire"—and also one that was ossified into an artifice. Her (non)corporeality and tone of voice made for a non-lively liveness and dismantled the playwright's authority with the non-referential and non-cathartic histrionics of her body become text. Mrs. Pat pathologized Paula's character, making it much more disturbing than a fairly typical case of a woman with a hypertrophic past. As Archer writes,

> . . . it seemed to me that Paula was not the ordinary upper-class cour-tesan, but simply a woman of diabolical temper, with whom life would have been impossible even if she had been chaste as the icicle that hangs on Dian's temple. (133)

Lund too remarks in his tract that "So powerful is Mrs. Campbell's portrayal of the real woman, that one finds oneself guessing at the origin of the jeal-ousy as though the instance before us were genuine and not fictitious" (7). By tracing an uncertain etiology to Paula's ill behavior, and debunking any intradiegetic prognosis or cure, Mrs. Pat Campbell imbued the world of the play with an infectious ill-being, or was it an uncontained jouissance? The critic of *Punch* recoiled from the character as "a *bete fauve* that should be under lock and key":

> she is loving, she is vulgar; she can purr, she can spit; she is gentle, she is violent; she has good impulses, and she is a fiend incarnate; she is affec-tionate, she is malicious; generous and trusting, selfish and suspicious; she is all heart and no soul. . . . [10]

Pinero had succeeded in a very modern and masterly orchestration of the public's discomfiture with his work. The *Era* of 29 May, 1893, reports the audience reaction to Paula's momentous recognition that Ellean's fiancé was her ex-lover, Hugh Ardale:

> As the full significance of the scene flashed upon the minds of the spec-tators, and quickened their pulses with horror and astonishment, the effect upon them was a study for any student of human nature. Some appeared to shrink, as if with pain, from the dreadful revelation; oth-ers, rigid with blank wonder, seemed hardly to comprehend it; fair faces became pale, and a visible shudder ran through the house.

Archer described it succinctly when he wrote "there is a certain aridity in its painfulness—it feels gritty to the mental palate" (131).

Despite his protestations to the contrary, Archer hankered after seeing the play again and again and the 27th December entry in the *World* sees him pondering once again on the pleasure-principle of a play which "cannot be called a *pleasant* play, an exhilarating and diverting entertainment":

> It is precisely this fact which renders its popularity so remarkable and encouraging. . . . One could almost parody the remark of the Edinburgh gallery-boy, and ask, "Whaur's your 'British Public' noo?"—the British Public which would accept nothing at the theatre but a mild narcotic after its day's work, which brought its young ladies of fifteen to the dress circle, and resented the slightest shock to their innocent ignorance, or ignorant innocence, which regarded the drama as a mere *chasse* to its after-dinner coffee, and demanded, not to think about life, but to leave its mind distracted from all serious thought whatsoever? (292–94)

What the success of *The Second Mrs Tanqueray* has done to prove, Archer acknowledges, is that there is a new and large stratum of theatergoers, "which takes its intelligence with it to the play" (294). Playwrights could now unravel or complicate tangled skeins of emotions that intrigued more than they amused, deferral and displacement could complicate the production of meaning and make spectatorial acts of recognition and transference tenuous and uncertain. Finally, melodramatic excess did not have to be easily expended in laughter. Theatergoers had finally come to terms with an obscure object of enjoyment that had to remain inscrutable for the desire to scrutinize, repeatedly, to be sustained.

Chapter Three

"Missed Encounters": Repetition, Rewriting, and Contemporary Returns to Charles Dickens's *Great Expectations*

"I love you, but, because inexplicably I love in you something more than you—the objet petit a*—I* mutilate *you."*

—Jacques Lacan, *The Four Fundamental Concepts of Psycho-Analysis*

Julian Barnes's *England, England,* true to the echolalic title, is about doubleness, more specifically the specular dualism of originality and replication. It questions the notion of authenticity as megalopolitan England atrophies and dies when beamed with the *idea* of England, and the image of a theme park named *England, England.* In his eternal quest for the top dollar and long yen, Jack Pitman—Sir Jack, an entrepreneur of the late-capitalist variety—fabricates England, England in the Isle of Wight, with fifty quintessences of Englishness (Royal Family, Big Ben, Man Utd., Class System, etc.). The French intellectual hired to hone the philosophical angle of this project sums it up to the coordinating committee as a *"rivalization* of reality." We prefer the replica to the original because it opens up endless possibilities of differential reproduction:

> We must demand the replica, since the reality, the truth, the authenticity of the replica is the one we can possess, colonize, reorder, find *jouissance* in, and, finally, if and when we decide, it is the reality which, since it is our destiny, we may meet, confront and destroy. (35)

The non-identical replica updates and problematizes the original. Representation, according to the Frenchman, is "an ironization and summation" of the thing represented: "A monochrome world has become Technicolor, a single croaking speaker has become wraparound sound" (55).

Sir Jack rewards such Platonic musings by paying the man in dollars instead of pounds, dollar being the replica, pound the prototype. Jack Pitman takes the discussion further. In offering a mediated image of England, he claims, "We are offering *the thing itself*" (59). A reservoir becomes a lake when it is built and positioned as a lake, and natural and man-made objects adopt it as such—it becomes *the thing itself*. In the novel, it becomes difficult to say what pre-exists repetition. Dr. Max, Official Historian of the project, observes later in the novel, "There is no prime moment," adding indignantly that "it is like saying that . . . a gibbon suddenly wrote Gibbon" (132). Replication in this sense does not follow the law of recurrence or the logic of compulsive returns, but is a mode of inventiveness, that, through its reiterative structure, mobilizes narrative instead of arresting it.

This chapter looks at rewritings of a well-made Victorian multi-plot novel completed in 1861, Charles Dickens's *Great Expectations,* to explore the dynamic between precursor and latecomer in terms of narrative operation. I am particularly interested in the remembering and reinterpretation of the literary canon, in acts of generative citation that bring the (Eurocentric) literary past to recurring life. The first section of the essay looks briefly at the Kathy Acker's and Sue Roe's extrapolations of the classic, and Alfonso Cuarón's 1998 film, *Great Expectations.* The second and last section is a reading of Peter Carey's brilliant Dickensian pastiche, *Jack Maggs.* What unites the late twentieth-century novels I have selected for this essay is a project of de-naturalizing, de-familiarizing, and problematizing "natural givens" in a master text. The constructedness of the literary artifact is seen, in these second comings, as analogous to the constructedness of identity categories and cultural formations: the work of rewriting then is to look awry at virtual pasts, interrupt collective identities and the habitual coherence of cultural experience, and confront the social discourse informing memorable acts of literature.

Is repetition a mode of recuperating loss, a ritual of control to cope with the reality-principle, as Freud suggested? Is it, as Lacan elaborates, a quest for lost pleasure through symbolic substitution, and a necessary condition of being in language? This essay erects an opposition between Freud's and Lacan's differing notions of repetition (mastery vs. alienation). The point where their readings come together is on the grounds of death, failure, or breakage. Repetition can only ever produce a certain kind of undoing. It is undeniable that rewriting is to writing, what writing is to speech—a supplement to a circumscribed entity, which demonstrates the latter's incompleteness and indeterminacy. While my examples are specific to particular novels, my thesis speaks, in a larger way, to the problem and anxiety of all modern literature: are all writers constrained to rework influence? If all writing is, in a Derridean sense, rewriting, then what more is there left to say?

In this chapter it is also my claim that repetition subscribes to the ethics of hysteria, which can be described as an ethics of deprivation and dispossession. The hysteric rejects a symbolic system dominated by the paternal metaphor, and sustains his or her radical alienation through a refusal of representation. As subject, the hysteric is divided and decentered, while as object s/he is the lack or nothing of desire, a flashing question mark, an ontological tease. As a mode of literary or aesthetic reception, hysteria prepares us for a series of departures from text and textuality to an alterity altogether uninhabitable by the materiality of the letter. While a (re)writing machine cannot be glibly equated to the pathological repetition manifested in symptoms, dreams, and parapraxes, it can be (approvingly) labeled hysterical in that it demonstrates the insistence and transference of labile, creative desire, and the impossibility of exemplification or closure. If the discourse of the hysteric is structured around what Bruce Fink calls "a unique configuration with respect to knowledge" (133), a perverse logic of loving *and* mutilating its epistemic objects, rewriting too simultaneously commemorates and disavows the privileged narratives that discursively constitute the canon. However, while hysteria is a useful heuristic for the theoretical questions the chapter is trying to pose, it may not itself be the answer so much as simply another example of the same cultural problem of a repetitive return to the real.

I. PRISONS OF MEANING

Writing of Charles Dickens's haunting of contemporary popular culture, Jay Clayton ascribes to his literary corpus a "grotesque, misshapen afterlife . . . as unsettling as the manias that animate some of Dickens's own creations: Miss Havisham in her decaying bridal dress, or Pip fantasizing about his great expectations" (147). Clayton's laundry list of maternity shops, dating services, hair salons, restaurants, and even *Saturday Night Live* skits named cringe-makingly after Dickens's *Great Expectations* reinforces his point about the continued imaginative stranglehold of this capacious phrase. Needless to say the novel itself has suffered a series of opportunistic symbolic appropriations and cinematic second comings. While David Lean adapted *Great Expectations* in the aftermaths of World War II to showcase his own brand of "colonial nostalgia" (Clayton 157), where a strong emotional bond between two men (Pip and Magwitch) across the cultural divide momentarily overcomes all socio-economic differences, Alfonso Cuarón's *Great Expectations*

(1998) incapacitates the dated center-periphery dialectic in favor of his protagonist's avowedly cosmopolitan epiphanies around the New York art scene. Cuarón moves the action from Victorian England to the Gulf Coast of America. Many of the characters of the Dickens original are renamed: Miss Havisham is Nora Dinsmoor (played by Anne Bancroft), Pip is Finn (Ethan Hawke plays him as an adult), and Magwitch is Lustig (Robert de Niro). "I am not gonna tell the story the way that it happened," drawls the voiceover, "I am gonna tell the way I remembered"—an ethos that well describes the project of "writing back" against a great English novel. What we get, however, is not so much a medium's awareness of its literary or cinematic past, or a palimpsest laid compulsively, mnemonically, on the original. Cuarón's recreation seems to have no motive beyond the fact that it takes advantage of technology to cinematically rethink Dickens's powerful narrative in MTV format. The plot rifles through fungible and forgettable contexts and characters, frequently losing itself in lush visuals. The bare bones of the Dickensian masterplot are retained: the chance encounter with a convict; the summons to an overgrown Gothic palazzo; an impossible and unamiable love object in Estella; Pip/Finn's traumatic yet exhilarating transition from country to city, here New York. The sun-dappled opening scene in Sarasota Bay, however, sets the mood for a cheerier tale—the critical reversal (the climax of Magwitch's discovery and recapture in the original) takes place not in the murky Thames estuary, but a preternaturally gleaming New York subway. Nora Dinsmoor has given up her melancholic wedding dress for vivid green ensembles, and has altogether "moved on." The huge masonry pile of "Paradiso Perduto" does not come to signify a complex of desire and fear for Finn—it provides instead a camp setting for Nora Dinsmoor's unremitting vulgarisms, and Finn's and Estella's dance to the tune of "Besame Mucho." Finn is untroubled by his repugnance towards his benefactor or about reinventing himself as an angsty artist in Soho by fabricating a genealogy that does little justice to his surrogate parent. The romance plot, unmoored by the irresolvable social problems posed by the original, shows artistic enervation or laziness at its worst. The ending is faithful to Dickens's second, more populist one for the novel. Cuarón does not so much look awry at literary and cinematic tradition: he simplemindedly sees through it.

Kathy Acker's *Great Expectations* (1982), by contrast, is a controlled chaos of genres, a parody *and* pastiche of the representational forms of (auto-biographical) narrative, fiction, drama, the epistolary novel, history, criticism, and poetry. The novel is a neurotic shape-shifter which cannibalizes older, mostly canonical texts: Dickens's novel by the same title, a porno-graphic novel, a Harlequin romance, excerpts of Greek history, a line from a

Keats letter. The narrator is identifiable as Pip, a woman, Rimbaud, Pasolini, O, or even Virginia Woolf's *Orlando*. As in her novel *Don Quixote*, Acker borrows the language, not themes of the precursor texts, to create—Acker's favored verb is "make"—something radical and novel out of agonistic textual encounters. To quote Acker from "A Few Notes,"

> . . . the world is always making itself. When you make fiction, you dip into this process. But no one, writer or politician, is more powerful than the world: you can make, but you don't create. Only the incredible egotism that resulted from a belief in phallic centricism could have come up with the notion of creativity. (33–34)

Acker claims in "A Few Notes on Two of My Books" that plagiarism helps her do "what gives the most pleasure: write" (34). Her technique of pseudo-plagiarism is random and free-associative, and also, contradictorily, strategic: she is interested in copying something without any reason ("Conversation" 12), but the plagiarism is also an attempt, she says, "to find writers who describe the particular place I want to get to" (Friedman 17). Acker's plagiarism serves to emphasize the derivativeness and mediatedness of all fiction; her technique of quotation and cross-quotation undermines the authenticity of the cloying confessional. The intent to damage the form and content of its originals, however, is somewhat diminished by the glib knowingness of the narrative voice: "one text must subvert (the meaning of) another text" (*Great Expectations* 15).

The traumatic *punctum* of Acker's heteroglossic *Great Expectations* is the author's mother's suicide. It is not mourned or memorialized, but experienced as a frame, within which the past is not over but *is*, and time is circular. This breakdown of temporality, or the temporal unification of past and future with one's present—an unmistakable symptom of (Acker's purchase of) the postmodern condition—leads to a breakdown of personal identity. The novel begins with the ending of the mother's life, and returns to it compulsively, unproductively. As the narrator says repetitively in the "Beginnings of Romance" section: "I realize that all my life is endings. Not endings, those are just events; but holes. For instance when my mother died, the 'I' I had always known dropped out. All my history went away" (64). The mother's suicide can be considered a logical copula that holds together various (unrelated) scenarios of oppression and victimization. The mother herself is interchangeably the object of courtly love and a victim of misogyny. Acker masterfully uses the mother's carnality—excessive, desired, tabooed—to recount real or fictional events. Her body, a splayed and violable female body, is both a site of resistance and out of control, schizophrenic, and oppressive. Around her, humans are always becoming animal: a cabby shoves his fist into a goat's face; females lullaby kids at their tits. The mother, "the most beautiful woman in the world" (7), is evoked after a graphic and lengthy description of rape and pillage. She is the "most disgusting thing in this world" (24) for being dispossessed and pitiably weak. In a sudden (and senseless) role reversal, the narrator's passive father becomes a rapist, the mother his prey. A violent primal scene plays out before the traumatized narrator:

> My father never beats my mother up. The father grabs a candle, the
> curly brownhaired soldier his red mouth rolling around the black meat
> takes out his knife [. . . .] jerks the sleepy young girl's thighs to him
> [. . . .] the sweat dripping off his bare strong chest wakes the young girl
> up, I walked into my parents' bedroom [. . .] I'm shocked[.] (13)

The pronoun reference leaves it unclear whether it is the mother or her young girl who is implicated in this phantasmagoric scene. The language dithers between meaning and the non-meaning of sights, sounds, the rude materiality of the text:

> Under the palmtrees the RIMAS seize and drag a fainted woman under
> a tent, a flushing-forehead blond soldier burning coals glaze his eyes
> his piss stops up his sperm grasps this woman in his arms, their hands
> their lips touch lick the woman's clenched face while the blond soldier's
> greasy wine-stained arm supports her body, the young girl RECOV-
> ERED[.] (15)

Acker borrows from Dickens's *Great Expectations* the almost exhibitionistic masochism of its hero. As Carol Siegel has observed, Acker's re-authored text "typifies her method of obsessively and starkly anti-erotically dwelling on what is usually suppressed in artistic depictions of sadomasochism, physical realities like infected sores and psychic realities like despair accompanying the certainty that [. . .] 'there's no hope of realizing what you want'" (9). In Dickens's novel, Pip's exquisite suffering in the hands of Estella metonymically connects her to a series of evil and unnatural dominatrixes—Miss Havisham, Mrs. Joe, and Magwitch's wild mistress—who are all eventually beaten into submission or written away as irrelevant. Acker points out the nexus between the idealization of women and vilification of prostitutes in Victorian society. She also seems to rebuke a carceral masochism not sublimated in art. Sexuality is coded, in very Freudian terms, as a kind of self-shattering not unlike masochism.

Pip inexplicably calls himself Peter, though this may have something to do with his conviction that "[the] logic way of talking (perceiving) is wrong" (24). He is benumbed and bereft of language or plot: "I feel I feel I feel I have no language, any emotion for me is a prison" (24). Character is defined by sexuality in Acker's nineteenth-century knock-off, but by making the gender of the masochistic narrator (who is both Pip and a woman) ambiguous and fluid, Acker "produces" a Victorian sexuality that is also uncannily postmodern. Like Dickens's protagonist, Pip claims to have great expectations, but unlike him is not obsessed about their origin or consequences, and does not need them as imaginative props for his escapist fantasies. Against the nineteenth-century model of developmental change, we have an aphasic subject fading away, sexual encounter after degrading sexual encounter. "There's no possibility that anyone'll love you anymore or that love matters" says he or she. "Because there's no hope of realizing what you want, you're a dead person and you're having sex" (51). In Dickens's *Great Expectations* the hero is systematically stripped of his fortunes and dreams, but, as Raymond Williams observes, this deprivation of identity is a kind of liberation "in which the most fantastic and idiosyncratic kinds of growth could come about" (53). Dickens's antiheroic and common Pip, who for the most part does not write his life story but is written, steps out of the *fictio* of his childhood and youth with the desire to articulate a life story. The autobiographical novel of endless reversals ends with the hope that Pip's belated authorship of his life will mark a rebeginning, not a return. In contrast, the hysterical protagonist of Acker's novel is dissatisfied, disgusted, and sick with desire: he or she ambivalently negotiates a cultural wasteland, where even language has been defeated by that which it could not speak for or of.

Sue Roe's *Estella: Her Expectations* (1982) rewrites the relationship of Dickens's Estella and her deranged guardian along the binaries of innocence and experience. If Estella dreams of a world "unstreaked by paint" (8), the dancer is a painted woman, a woman with color, first glimpsed in the novel as a pair of scarlet-tipped feet resting on a window ledge. Estella, who has skated on surfaces so far, and sauntered through life like a *flâneuse*, is seduced by the promise of depth, or depths of decadence, held out by the unseen "interior interiors" of the dancer's decaying house. The dancer, like Miss Havisham, is a woman with a past, but one who seeks to mitigate and sublimate it in her art. Estella likes to visualize the "dancer dancing towards the death wheels of some strain, some painful memory" (56)—in her mind, the fantasy of autonomy is inescapably linked to a repetition of pain. [T]hat dress," all yellowing lace and thin black threads, with small spiders sewn into it, is a relic of the past, an intractable remainder: "whatever the story you invented for that dress, it would still have a strange and mysterious meaning of its own" (48). The dancer's aberrant relationship with her reference is symbolized by a tarnished mirror—how does she know who she is, wonders Estella, ontologically implicated as she is in a non-reflecting surface and the folds of a dead dress? Even the jewels on the dancer's rings are opaque, non-representing. They become metaphors for Estella's preferred mode of aesthetic representation: "the half light, the scarlet and the damson, the spidery light" (80) of an imaginative vision, innocent, as it were, of meaning.

In Roe's novel, Estella wants to play at being Miss Havisham, caught in the non-productive, non-differential repetition of a wounding past. She however feels paralyzed to act out her dreams, and fails to even transcribe them. Dickens's Pip appears in the novel as archetypal child, prefiguring Estella's playful escapades into art and literature, which are chastised by her friend Mercy: "Look for something outside your wretched mirror. Realize there's a very large framework out there. Take something on" (88). In the Dickens original, Pip's role as paralyzed witness actualizes—in a sublimated narrative form—Miss Havisham's perverse fantasy. In the tale of Estella's expectations, she (Estella) catatonically views scenes of love and perversion before retreating to an underworld adrift from social reality, a fate eerily similar to that of Miss Havisham in the original. Her consciousness is punctuated by fugue-like states, a "hallucinatory no-man's land between sleep and waking" (107). Her dreams immure no positivity, no vision of a viable identity, but circle around a terrible dereliction: "an absence—a space unfilled by any form that might represent Estella" (116). There are echoes of Marguerite Duras's *The Ravishing of Lol Stein* here: Lol (the name a palindrome, like 'Pip') is a prototype of the voyeuristic, yet unseeing Estella. As in Pip's tradition of courtly love, Lol posits her desire as impossible; unlike Pip she is ultimately ruined by the absence of love's returning gaze. Sue Roe's ending seems to suggest the failure of sublimation, and the subsequent darkening of desire into pathology. The plague of phantasms, rich grist for art and literature, has become an end in itself: Estella is hooked on formless dreams like the insects in the dancer's wedding dress. The novel ends with Estella in an unnarratable and nonnarrativized state, settling herself to watch the inscrutable objects of her love.

II. MISTAH DICKENS—HE DEAD

In his 1997 novel *Jack Maggs*, Peter Carey borrows the character of Abel Magwitch from Charles Dickens's *Great Expectations*. Jack Maggs is a harking back, not just to Dickens's work, but also to the life of Dickens or the life of Dickens as a (biographical) text. Carey's novel is best described as a departure from its putative origin—not a return *to* (the past), or a return *of* (the repressed), but a return *from* the London and the social order pickled in Dickens's novel, with a desire to make real its substantial but unlived-out life.

In Dickens's text, Magwitch is associated with a shameful, hypertrophic past that the hero of the mobility narrative is trying to flee from. It is, however, a past that is dynamically interconnected with the present, and, in a curious way, facilitates the conditions of that flight. In his earliest conception of the novel, Dickens intended that *Great Expectations* would revolve around Pip's relationship with Magwitch, and it does so structurally.[1] If, in the novel's imaginary, Miss Havisham moves in a bizarre, self-enclosed circling around arrested time, Magwitch stands for the regenerative cycle and circulation of life which animates its symbolic structure. He is the occasion for Pip's "first most vivid and broad impression of the identity of things" (35) in the church graveyard in the beginning of the novel, the scene, as Said elaborates in *Beginnings,* of "Pip's origin as a novelistic character [. . .] rooted in the death of his parents" (97–98). He returns to Pip in the thirty-ninth chapter, after an absence of fifteen years, to climactically link past with the future, high expectations with low origins, criminality with gentility, the nightmarish marshes to the nightmarish metropolis. His reappearance in the last third of the novel triggers off a chain of events that revise the terms of Pip's *bildungsroman:* he turns out to be Pip's benefactor, Molly's lover, Estella's father, and the ex-partner of Compeyson, the man who was Miss Havisham's ex-fiancé.

"My father's family name being Pirrip, and my christian name being Philip, my infant tongue could make of both names nothing longer or more explicit than Pip. So, I called myself Pip, and came to be called Pip" (35)—these are the famous first lines of Dickens's novel. Pip's incipient subjectivity is tied up with language, but language threatens to constitute him as a void to be filled with phantasms and false signs. "The tracing of the name—which he has already distorted in application to self—involves a misguided attempt to remotivate the graphic symbol, to make it directly mimetic, mimetic specifically of origin," states Peter Brooks. This is a novel of "loss of origin, misreading, and the problematic of identity," he cautions (116). Pip's identity is grounded in unstable foundations, the loss of a family, and an act of unwilled charity towards the convict. Pip shores up Byzantine mental constructions that help him to entail affiliation with Satis House—the source, he thinks, of his great expectations.

> She reserved it for me to restore the desolate house, admit the sunshine into the dark rooms, set the clocks going and the cold hearths a blazing,

tear down the cobwebs, destroy the vermin—in short do all the shining
deeds of the young Knight of romance [. . .]. Estella was the inspiration of it, and the heart of it, of course. (253)

Pip's compromise with reality is paralleled, in this novel, in Wemmick's castle
at Walworth, complete with fake battlements and a drawbridge, and the poi-
soned interiority of Miss Havisham's Satis House: monuments to solipsism and
self-enclosed fantasy, from which only Pip is lucky enough to escape. This free
improvisation of his genealogy meets its first resistance in Miss Havisham. She
tweaks desire in Pip through Estella only to take delight in their subsequent
frustration. Pip enters fugue-like states and hallucinates about Miss Havisham
hanging by the neck (93–94). He is beside himself in appetency and terror, in
appetency born of terror: "I at first ran from it, and then towards it" (94). In
a bizarre wish fulfillment—in the tremendous fire scene—Pip gets to forgive
Miss Havisham, and aid the full-scale conflagration of her repressed affect.
Miss Havisham goes up in the ecstasy of emotional recognition, even as Pip
literally saves her from the flames. She succumbs to "nervous shock" and not
actual burns (435) in an expiatory death: the cake is destroyed, the old wedding dress burnt to ashes, the rotting chamber cleansed by fire.

Pip's "ecstasy of unhappiness" reaches a crescendo with Estella:

> You are part of my existence, part of myself. You have been in every
> line I have ever read [. . .]. You have been in every prospect I have ever
> seen [. . .]. Estella, to the last hour of my life, you cannot choose but
> remain part of my character, part of the little good in me, part of the
> evil. (378)

We suddenly see Estella for what she is: "the embodiment of every grace-
ful fancy" (378), woman-manipulated-as-sign, a linguistic object projected
on the text by the sweeping "you are part of my existence." Pip as controlling subject has introjected the apostrophized object: "you cannot choose but
remain part of my character." He hunts down Estella's lowly parentage, and
the power/knowledge of the purloined story of her birth affects his remark-
able self-possession in the revised ending of the novel. Estella's secret does
not involve her at all; it is part of the discourse that first inscribes and then
reads her. In the ending Dickens decided to publish, we have in her chastised
and impoverished body a moral ending for Pip's story, a trope that unites self
and sign with "no shadow of another parting" (493).

Lacan sees language as a signifying chain—"rings of a necklace that is a
ring in another necklace made of rings" (*Écrits* 153). "Pause you who read this,"

Pip says, "and think for a moment of the long chain of iron or gold, or thorns or flowers, that would never have bound you, but for the formation of the first link on one memorable day" (101). Magwitch is the first link of the serial articulations of Pip's tale. He is what Lacan calls "the past in its real form":

> not the physical past whose existence is abolished, nor the epic past as it has become perfected in the work of memory, nor the historic past in which man finds the guarantor of his future, but the past which reveals itself reversed in repetition. (*Écrits* 103)

Pip is afflicted by this past, which refuses to be petrified as memory, or super-seded and subsumed in the future. The early encounter with Magwitch gives rise to "inexplicable feeling[s]" (403) and phantasmagoric delusions in Pip: it accounts for his acute disconcertment when he visits Newgate; Estella, boast-ing of not having "a heart to be stabbed in or shot in" (259) makes him associ-ate her with the criminal nexus of Newgate-Molly-Magwitch; the death masks of two hanged convicts in Jaggers's office hold his gaze; Miss Havisham, touch-ing her hands to her chest, evokes the memory of Magwitch's terrifying story of a young man who fed on the hearts and livers of small boys. The "dead hare hanging by the heels" (13) in Mrs. Joe's kitchen, and the hanging visions of Miss Havisham are both displacements of his early imagining of Magwitch hanging from a gibbet. Pip's final reconciliation with Magwitch—and his idea of Magwitch—follows a regime of disillusionments: his acknowledgement of Magwitch's connections with Miss Havisham and Estella, his arrest for debt, delirious illness, and reunion with his childhood companions, Joe Gargery and Biddy. Pip becomes a benefactor, and makes Herbert a gentleman: he has exploded the self-enclosed self to participate in an economy of circulation. Pip's "smart without a name, that needed counteraction" (92) can finally be elabo-rated, named, and shared—it becomes the novel Dickens has him narrate.

It is impossible not to see in Pip's projections, Dickens's childhood trauma—"the secret agony of my soul" (qtd.: in Forster 2:26), the abjection of the debtor's prison and the blacking factory—and his subsequent inven-tion of a comfortable middle-class childhood for himself. Peter Ackroyd, his biographer, sees *Great Expectations* as a study in self-knowledge:

> It is in any event a book of great psychological accuracy and observa-tion, as if Dickens were secretly examining himself as he writes, analys-ing the nature of passion, of hypocrisy, of psychological meanness, all those things 'low and small' of which Pip eventually realizes himself to be guilty. (899)

And, who is Magwitch but Dickens's Muse, whom he followed from hospital to warehouse to morgue, and in night patrols with the police to the dens of criminals and prostitutes?[2] Dickens was almost constantly in pain while writing this novel, suffering from what he termed "facial neuralgia," which vanished the day he finished his work (Ackroyd 900).

Peter Brooks reads *Great Expectations* with Freud's *Beyond the Pleasure Principle,* using Freud's theorization of repetition to understand the functioning of the novel. Freud identifies the compulsion to repeat as the expression of a death instinct. "The impulse to work over in the mind some overpowering experience so as to make oneself master of it," Freud states, becomes "a compulsion to repeat—something that seems more primitive, more elementary, more instinctual than the pleasure principle which it over-rides" (SE 18: 16, 23). Freud begins with the child's *fort/da* game of wresting control over privation, and then moves to a discussion of primary processes where energy seeks instant gratification. Repetition is what binds and rations energy, and postpones its discharge: mastery springs from this postponement. As Brooks points out, repetition compulsion and the death instinct ultimately service the pleasure principle, though they are more primitive: the eschewal of immediate pleasure ensures "that the ultimate pleasurable discharge will be more complete" (101–2).

Freud's "masterplot" for organic life, according to Brooks, is an energetic model for narrative plot. We are all moving towards death, just as the elaboration of plot is end-driven. Repetition links the origin with the end, and is a deviance, detour, and delay of fulfillment. As Brooks states so eloquently,

> We emerge from reading *Beyond the Pleasure Principle* with a dynamic model that structures ends (death, quiescence, nonnarratability) against beginnings (Eros, stimulation into tension, the desire of narrative) in a manner that necessitates the middle as detour, as struggle toward the end under the compulsion of imposed delay, as arabesque in the dilatory space of the text. (107–8)

In Brooks's reading, *Great Expectations* dramatizes the ambiguities of repetition: is repetition sameness or difference? Is it a return to or a return of? Pip's returns *to* origins (to Satis House, for example) and the returns *of* the repressed (as in the repetition of the convict material) seem to attest to Freud's insight that we cannot but repeat the unmastered past till we have incorporated the end in relation to the beginning. "We are condemned to repetition, rereading, in the knowledge that what we discover will always be that there was nothing to be discovered" (142).

Freud's model of repetition as a symbolic enactment of unconscious material from the past cannot be easily applied to the phenomenon of rewriting and revisiting canonical works. *Great Expectations* is an unlikely cause of childhood trauma, and the superior artistic production that is *Jack Maggs* makes it difficult to treat it as a symptom, an inscrutable kernel of enjoyment that mocks the absolutism of the signifier. However, we can read literary rewriting as an *intentional* act of wish fulfillment that emphasizes the retro-activity of meaning. The logic of this deferred action is well-captured in the temporal insights of Lacanian psychoanalysis. As Slavoj Žižek states, "instead of the linear, immanent, necessary progression according to which meaning unfolds itself from some initial kernel, we have a radically contingent process of retroactive production of meaning" (*The Sublime Object of Ideology* 102). The forms and content literary rewritings seek to find, or refind, are often phantasmatic in nature. They look back in anger or longing for objects always already lost.

Peter Carey's *Jack Maggs,* like Dickens's *Great Expectations,* is about the writing of a novel. The author in question, Tobias Oates, is not the narrator, nor is the novel *The Death of Maggs,* written by the end of *Jack Maggs,* the narrative we read. The plot is an elaborate mediation between Dickens's *Great Expectations* and Oates's *Death of Maggs,* letting us glimpse at the "real" life of Maggs which fiction must lie, falsify, and invent around in order to reveal. Oates is Dickens himself: Cockney, flamboyant, ambitious, obsessive, impatient to mire lived experience in unhysterical detail and the wordy and unreal brilliance of his art. And Maggs is Magwitch, the recalcitrant object of Dickens's/Oates's aesthetic, and as we shall see later, what survives its maltreatment.

Carey's novel begins with Jack Maggs's return to London to meet his surrogate English "son" whose great expectations he has funded, with wealth gained in the colonies. Like Pip's convict, he is "whipped and worried and drove" (*GE* 360) into criminality, and deported to Australia, where, after his conditional pardon, he makes a fortune from clay. He arrives at Mr. Phipps' residence at 27 Great Queen Street, to find no one home "but draughts and mice" (8) and decides to accept gainful employment in Mr. Percy Buckle's house next door as a footman. Mr. Buckle, a Clerkenwell grocer, has come into money late in life, and enjoys its sweets: the complete set of Gibbon's *Decline and Fall,* distinguished company, and the saucy kitchen maid, Mercy Larkin. It is in this household that Maggs meets Tobias Oates, the increasingly popular author of comic tales and creator of Captain Crumley and Mrs Morefallen.

Tobias Oates lives with his wife and her younger sister, whom he loves, in domestic bliss fringed with anarchic desires. Like Dickens, he scours the wondrous and awful city by foot, from townhouse to rookery

morgue; in one of the pigeonholes in his meticulously neat study is a
ief's hand purchased from a shop in Whitechapel, while another holds
e death mask of John Sheppard, hanged at Tyburn in 1724. The "Crimi-
Mind" beckons him to be its "first cartographer" (89). From a chance
counter with Maggs, Oates knows his secret—the flight from New
ith Wales—and enters into a pact where he will, through mesmerism,
sack Maggs's unconscious and construct stories *post factum*, in exchange
help to locate Henry Phipps. In counterpoint to this ungenerous model
of creativity, Maggs embarks on a storytelling of his own, in the form of
personal letters to his dear protégé, heartrending tales of shame and terror
from his dreary and damaged childhood.

Jack Maggs out-Dickens a Dickensian work. Ma Britten, Captain Constable, Percy Buckle are urban neurotics: Ma Britten sells miscarriage pills,
Captain Constable is a suicidal homosexual, and Percy Buckle alarmingly
morphs from a harmless bookworm to a homicidal maniac. The mud flats
and scavengers of *Our Mutual Friend,* the protracted and inscrutable legacies
of *Bleak House,* the girl prostitutes of *David Copperfield,* the social casualties
of the city's orphanages and ghettoes and the ubiquitous gallows of *Oliver
Twist,* all come together like fragments of emotive memory in Carey's novel.
Maggs's elaborate quest is emplotted against this ghoulish background. In
Dickens's novel, Magwitch is redeemed in the end by a contrite Pip, who
sees in him "my benefactor, and who had felt affectionately, gratefully, and
generously, towards me with great constancy through a series of years" (456–
57). Maggs, however, is shot by a monstrously selfish Phipps, and saved by
Mercy Larkin, Buckle's maid and one-time lover. He returns to Australia
and dies, years later, "in a musty high-ceilinged bedroom above the flood-
brown Manning River [. . .] with his weeping sons and daughters crowded
around his bed" (328). The serialization of *The Death of Maggs* begins three
years after his death.

In *Great Expectations,* Magwitch is used as what Joseph A. Hynes calls
the "Magwitch motif," a contingency that influences Pip's self-discovery and
coming of age.[3] In *Jack Maggs* Carey refuses us the comfort of the Oedipal paradigm: there is no castrating father without the guilty son. In Pip's
absence—or phantom presence, for he peoples Maggs's nightmares—one can
no longer valorize metalanguage over language by turning to the false objectivity of myth, literature, or psychoanalysis. Carey fixes our gaze on Maggs's
lash-scarred back in an episode of animal magnetism in Oates's house:

> Jack Maggs shed his jacket, then his silk ruff and shirt, and then the coarse
> wool singlet, and stood before them, naked to the waist. [. . .] As Lizzie

> Warriner raised her eyes, she gasped at the sea of pain etched upon the footman's back, a brooding sea of scars, of ripped and tortured skin. (86)

The objective of the Mesmeric Exhibition is to "drag the demons out of Master Maggs" with magnets (80): pick apart the convict's unconscious, read and diligently expound it by a Sherlock Holmes-ish waking consciousness. Carey is at pains to point out that the material signs of suffering— Maggs's "restless limbs, his twisted mouth," his fear of flogging and the blistering sun, thirst and pain—are analyzed by Oates with all the empathy of, say, a literary critic. However, if Tobias Oates secures the right to be "the archaeologist of this mystery . . . the surgeon of this soul" (54), Maggs does not succumb easily to this shamanistic power. He feels burgled, eviscerated, narrated:

> 'You are filled with Phantoms, Master Maggs. It is these Phantoms who cause you such distress. Did you know that? Do you know what hobgoblins live inside your head like beetles in a fallen log?'
> 'But how did you make me speak?' cried the visitor.
> . . . .
> 'Last night you were a Somnambulist.'
> 'Whatever it is called, it is a terrible thing, Sir, for a man to feel his insides all exposed to public view [. . .].'
> 'Would you rather keep the pain?'
> 'I would have it back ten times over, if my secrets came with it.' (46)

The trauma of the Jack Maggs's middle passage between *there* and *here, now,* cannot be commemorated in Oates's literary project.

Maggs, however, chooses to remember and recover his history in epistolary form. He writes in invisible ink—his art is "distrustful" of interpellation (74). It is a "different type of story" (74) the inverse (written right to left) of the one Tobias is plotting, in that "it kept its secrets to itself" (158). The letters narrate his blighted childhood with Ma Britten, purveyor of "belly-ache sausages" and "Dr Britten's Cock Spur Pills for Female Disorders" (209) and a life-denying force; her partner, the thief Silas Smith; her son Tom; and Tom's daughter Sophina. We come to know that the convict's surname, Maggs, is not a patronymic—like Pip, he too has a false name, slapped on him by his foster mother Mary Britten "who believed I talked too much" (75). Sophina and he work hard as burglars, and make love in the scene of crime: "'Twere the sweetest thing in all my life, to go burgling with Sophina and to flirt with the great dangerous web of sleep which came down to claim us afterwards" (216). Mary Britten discovers Sophina's pregnancy soon afterwards, and a home remedy is administered with alacrity. Maggs's autobiography reaches breaking point when he remembers the fetus, damaged and cast-out, in the collapsing drain, surrounded by excrement and rottenness: "There lay our son—the poor dead mite was such a tiny thing. I could have held him in my hand. And on his queerly familiar little face, a cruel and dreadful cut. Cannot write more at this time" (241). Later in his life, when he lets Tobias Oates ransack his secrets, Maggs returns to the traumatic scene to address his incomprehension. Oates has magnetized him, and is decoding the dialect of his delirium: "With Jack Maggs, there was always an obstacle—a wall, a moat, a bridge—some impediment which must be crossed to enter the castle of the Criminal Mind" (201). Oates wears down the resistance, brick by brick, and the somnambulist releases "a wail, so long and dreadful that the writer, listening to it, bowed his head and shut his eyes" (202). There, on the other side of the wall, is a little boy lying in a ditch. "My *babe*. My babe is dead" (204).

Jack Maggs's letters do not reach the intended addressee. Mercy Larkin saves Maggs from Phipp's fire, and rehabilitates him with his real offspring in Australia. While there is no character like Mercy in *The Death of Maggs,* it is she who makes possible the publication of Jack Maggs's letters to Henry Phipps. The sliding, and crucial address, upon which all the unread and unreadable messages converge, is that of the reader. We are enjoined to read this purloined text with caution and unsentimental charity.

Carey's homage to Dickens, in this retelling, bristles with passionate indictment and a vexed author-to-author filiation. The "tortured beast" (325) of *Jack Maggs* is not its eponymous hero but the diminutive Tobias Oates, Carey's predecessor Dickens. To the jaded modern reader, anaesthetized to the shock of conceptual art, where a urinal in a New York gallery is called "fountain" and a pickled shark becomes a memento mori, Carey delivers a chilling warning about the exploitative nature of a process in which objects become found objects and works of art. The literary marketplace is Oates's playground. The irresponsibility with which he rifles through the creatures from Jack Maggs's past comes with the territory:

> [H]e had a premonition of the true majesty of the work he would one day write. And how did he value this portent? Why, like a pawnbroker. He examined this great novel with his jeweller's glass. He might contrive to sell the copyright of such a work, and sell it entire, today, with not a word yet written. (198–99)

In yet another perspicacious observation, Carey links the serialization of (Dickens's) novels with the elusiveness of an end story. Tobias himself is desperate enough to reject the traditional media of writing—inspiration and ink—for the bulky apparatus of mesmerism. His long-suffering wife, Mary, is the first to register this loss of nerve: "You never needed magnets before. You used an ink and pen. You made it up, Toby. Lord, look at the people you have made. Mrs Morefallen. Did you need magnets to dream her up?" (118).

From around 1838, Dickens was deeply interested in mesmerism, and part of a movement that later influenced hypnotists like Ambrose Liébeault, Jean-Martin Charcot, and Sigmund Freud (Kaplan 133). He participated in mesmerist exhibitions, and practiced mesmerism himself: trances, fantasies, dreams, a panoply of conversion disorders lent themselves to the secondary elaboration of language and literature. *Jack Maggs* is about the seductiveness and fallaciousness of this experiment. Psychology is nothing without language, or stylistics, but that also means that its glib diagnostic suppositions are metaphorical, not literal truths. Tobias Oates sees in Jack Maggs "[a] memory I can enter, and leave" (87). However, the more fathomable Maggs's body is, the more indecipherable its mysteries become:

> [H]e memorized the hard shine to Jack Maggs's skin as it cleaved close to the bones of his cheek and jaw. He would use those bones, perhaps tomorrow. On the following day he would return for those deeper, more painful items which must still be cut free from the softer tissue of Jack Maggs's memory. (178)

Maggs's pain offers ferocious resistance through its intangibility, a particular that defers the whole. Oates "feared he had done something against the natural order, had unleashed demons he had no understanding of, disturbed some dark and dreadful nest of vermin" (203). Language cannot fully capture or kill this alterity:

> Tobias reflected on how he was to lay this Phantom to rest forever. He had by now forgotten, if he ever knew, that this wraith was his own invention, a personification of pain that he had planted in the other's mind. He commanded the Somnambulist to describe the figure that haunted him. [. . .] his purpose was to make his subject concentrate upon the phantom, and then, by some violent strategy he had not yet imagined, to cast him for ever, like swine, into the sea. (203)

Jack Maggs shares in Hegel's notion of the imperfect correspondence between the mind and objective reality, meaning and living, and powerfully dramatizes the detrimental consequences of not minding the gap. Tobias's life becomes a tableau of horrors: his mesmerism kills a man, his illicit love affair ends in pregnancy, abortion, and death, and most unfortunate of all, "the Criminal Mind [becomes] repulsive to his own imagination" (303). At the end of the novel he mourns the premature deaths of his lover Lizzie (from an overdose of Mrs Britten's miscarriage pills, procured by Maggs), of the homunculus that would have been their love-child, and of the manuscripts from the Maggs project. Stoking the fire that engulfs the pages of his unfinished work, and the bloody sheets from his sister-in-law's deathbed, Tobias sees Maggs "flowering, threatening, poisoning" (326), and plots a new novel in revenge. This Jack Maggs—*The Death of Maggs*—"was, of course, a fiction" (326).

III. NOVEL REWRITINGS

At the heart of experience, according to Lacan, is the insistence of the real— that which cannot be symbolized, a "petrified forest of enjoyment," as Žižek states ("The Truth Arises from Misrecognition" 203) which meaning cannot infiltrate. Lacan links repeating with the limit posed by the opacity of the real:

> An adequate thought, *qua* thought, at the level at which we are, always avoids—if only to find itself again later in everything—the same thing. Here, the real is that which always comes back to the same place—to the place where the subject in so far as he thinks, where the *res cogitans,* does not meet it. (*Four Fundamental Concepts* 49)

The unthinkable, unspecularizable real elicits desire but will not be dialecticized or objectified by it. It engenders repetition, and a series of misrecognitions. Lacan returns to Freud's celebrated example of repetition, the *fort-da* game, to revise its meaning:

> The activity as a whole symbolizes repetition, but not at all that of some need that might demand the return of the mother, and which would be expressed quite simply in a cry. It is the repetition of the mother's departure as cause of a *Spaltung* in the subject—overcome by the alternating game, *fort-da,* which is a *here* or *there,* and whose aim, in its alternation, is simply that of being the *fort* of a *da,* and the *da* of a *fort.* It is aimed at what, essentially, is not there, *qua* represented. (*Four Fundamental Concepts* 62–63)

The cause of repetition, I repeat, is a lost cause. Repetition is repetition of what is missed (cognitively). The function of the child's exercise with the small bobbin, "refers to an alienation, and not to some supposed mastery": repetition is endless, says Lacan, and reveals "the radical vacillation of the subject" (239). Lacan situates our relation to the real not as a simple matter of seeing or knowing it, but as an urgent responsibility, or what he describes as an ethical relation to the real. The real functions as an encounter, "insofar as it may be missed, insofar as it is essentially the missed encounter" (*Four Fundamental Concepts* 55). The missing of the real is also an encounter, in fact it is the only ethical encounter with the real: a feeling of radical destitution transmits the otherness of the real, and the estranged encounter with that otherness.

In Freudian analysis, repetition is linked to incomprehension. We return to the past to address what we haven't understood, and overwrite through representation what seems heterogeneous and inassimilable otherwise. Repetition characterizes the drives that engineer life, both pertaining to the pleasure principle, and to what is beyond it. The aim of organic life, Freud observes, is not evolution but regression and return to the inorganic—the outcome of life is death. Lacan's view of the repetitive structure of the symbolic is similarly dire. According to him, repetition is in fact the signifier's repeated failure to designate itself. Lacan identifies as the "real" an order of effects that resist symbolization, and remain as a counterpoint, breaking the chains of signification. The impossibility of signifying the real is matched, in Lacan's conception of language, with repeated attempts to see it transversally through language, or at least inscribe its impossibility. As Jean François Lyotard says of Joyce's *Ulysses*, it is all about an odyssey of consciousness: the mind acquires "its final identity, its self-knowledge, by exposing itself [. . .] to the risk of losing itself" (126). The game is repeated endlessly with the hope, but without the certainty, of grasping that which eludes it. Each reworking of the literary and linguistic investiture of Dickens's novel takes on the real insofar as the real is an impossible, non-narrativized, unrealized potential in the narrative that generates a series of failed encounters.

The novels by Carey, Acker, and Roe discussed here playfully blur the boundary between new and old, tradition and individual talent, and the Derridean categories of inventiveness and programmability. They renew old pleasures and reopen old wounds by their deliberate affiliation to familiar texts. This form of narrative mimicry pries open what D. A. Miller identifies as the inexhaustible "narratable" element of well-concluded novels: "the various incitements to narrative, as well as the dynamic ensuing from such incitement" (x). The narratable is never quite used up in the inexorable movement of plot toward expedient endings. Rewritings pit the narrated against traces of the narratable, brushing aside an immanent and linear production of meaning for one that is contingent and retroactively thrust upon. Freud states in the *Three Essays on Sexuality* that "[t]he finding of an object is in fact a refinding of it" (SE 7, 222), alluding to an interminable psychic process of (re)enacting forever lost scenarios like the illicit mother-child dyad. With reference to literary rewritings we could say that the refinding of an object is in fact a finding of it: it has the brio and insouciance of an act of invention.

In the psychoanalytic scene, one repeats in order to remember, but what one seeks to recover never *was*. Since the lost object is phantasmatic and hypothetical in nature, its true meaning can never correspond with approximations in language: something escapes literalization and disturbingly returns. Lacan calls this remainder "object (a)," and Bruce Fink describes it succinctly as "the leftover of that process of constituting an object, the scrap that evades the grasp of symbolization" (Fink 94). Lacan links object (a) to love, which is not just a sum of parts of the loved object. We love in the other something that exceeds his gifts and qualities: the belated effect of a statement, the lingering of a voice, "something more" and self-alienating in him. And we disfigure beloved objects to make them intelligible, to activate transference, to simply connect. For the hysteric, object (a) is the truth—the hysteric's discourse engages with that preponderant, objectal "thingness" in the subject, which resists representation. The hysteric is a belligerent subject, forever questioning the mandate that locates her in the network of intersubjective relations. Žižek calls hysteria "the effect and testimony of a failed interpellation" (*Sublime Object,* 113), the failure of the subject to identify with the symbolic order. The hysteric's desire exceeds her demand, and her utterance falls short of her enunciation: to quote Žižek again, the hysteric position can be articulated as "'I'm demanding this of you, but what I'm really demanding of you is to refute my demand because this is not it!'" (112). The hysteric is after the phantasmatic surplus-object, the *objet a,* the real of *jouissance* which language cannot pin down. (Re)writing replicates this pattern of desire in that it, too, strains toward a traumatic impossibility, something that has to be addressed if not symbolized, repeated if not recuperated in transcendental categories.

Rewriting as re-creation dislocates the hierarchical relationship between the original and the replica, the donor and receiver of forms. Since it is not merely imitation but a transformative and transgressive reimagining, postmodern rewriting, to borrow Else Ribeiro Pires Vieira's astute observation on the poetics of (postcolonial) translation, "unleashes the epistemological challenge of discontinuity but reunites threads into a new fabric; a translation project which murders the father, means in his absence yet reveres him by creating a continued existence for him in a different corporeality" (97). Working with inherited material, the rewritings of *Great Expectations* are also unwritings, which worry their precursor's critical engagement with the place and claims of marginalized alterity. They unfailingly raise and sometimes replicate the problem of representation, where the aesthetic object is explicated in a conceptual framework. Each takes literature to a new breaking point as it strains harder to achieve shared language or dialogue between different peoples, rationalities, and modalities. Lacan insists that the subject must come to *be* amid foreignness, battling an out of joint reality. As Carey demonstrates in his sympathetic portrayal of Dickens's outlaw Magwitch, the artist too must engage with unending responsibility with an outside or otherness that rudely provokes art but will not be usurped by it. Lacan's term for unconscious repetition is "acephalic" or "headless" (*The Seminar of Jacques Lacan, Book II* 167). In these rewritings we have an "acting out" of unconscious and repressed material in the precursor texts, a repetition that is headless to some extent, but largely a cognitive and emotional intervention that seeks to recover lost memory by writing it backwards and to constitute the past through deferred action. This *mise-en-scène* of postmodern rewriting demonstrates hysteria's anomie or, more positively, its naughty secret: there is nowhere to return to, and nothing to remember, for what it "repeats" compulsively is that which was never experienced.

Chapter Four

Broken English: Neurosis and Narration in Pat Barker's *Regeneration* Trilogy

"I—I—" he stammered.

—Virginia Woolf, *Mrs Dalloway*

Melville's Billy Budd had "just one thing amiss in him," goes the narrative, "an occasional liability to a vocal defect" (53). Billy's linguistic breakdown on board the H. M. S. *Bellipotent*—his "stutter or even worse" (53)—precipitates a near-mutiny, mobilizing the unspoken collective murmurs of the common sailors on the ship against the authoritarian Captain Vere. As the plot goes, Billy the sailor, possessor of great masculine beauty, falls foul of the ship's master-at-arms and head of police surveillance, the sociopathic John Claggart. We are told that Claggart's antipathy to Billy Budd is spontaneous and profound, though unprovoked by any offending word, deed, or trait as such. In the climactic scene, Billy, convulsed by his speech impediment, unintentionally delivers a fatal blow to Claggart in response to the latter's false incriminations. Their final struggle is coded in almost clinical terms, prefiguring agonistic analytic scenarios between neurotic patients and neurasthenic doctors. Melville describes Claggart as confronting Billy "with the measured step and calm collected air of an asylum physician approaching in the public hall some patient beginning to show indications of a coming paroxysm" (98). Billy's muscular and nervous paroxysm following Claggart's accusation and Captain Vere's injunction to respond to it, results in a fatal "tongue-tie" (98):

> while the intent head and entire form straining forward in an agony
> of ineffectual eagerness to obey the injunction to speak and defend
> himself, gave an expression to the face like that of a condemned vestal

priestess in the moment of being buried alive, and in the first struggle
against suffocation. [. . .] The next instant, quick as the flame from a
discharged cannon at night, his right arm shot out. (98–99)

In *Strange Talk,* an excellent study of the linguistic psychology of Gilded
Age America, Gavin Jones suggests that Billy's linguistic affliction is contagious: "*Billy Budd* constructs the disturbing possibility that the forms of social
power, in addition to subaltern forces of resistance, are contaminated by a
single linguistic disease" (80). According to Jones, Billy Budd's stutter must
be assessed in the context of the prevalent neurasthenic climate in Melville's
America, and with direct reference to "American Nervousness," a catch-all
term coined by neurologist George M. Beard, to classify neurotic reactions to
urbanization, capitalism, and social mobility in the Gilded Age. Put simply,
people were nervous because they had reached the acme of private and public
success. Beard catalogued five main causes of American nervousness: steam-
power, the periodical press, the telegraph, the sciences, and the mental activity of women. Melville too imaginatively configured the Nore Mutiny as an
epidemic disease: "the distempering irruption of contagious fever in a frame
constitutionally sound, and which anon throws it off" (55). If we extend this
analogy to the hysterical stammer, it may be seen as a virus that infiltrates the
healthy idioms and articulations of dominant discourse.

Billy is an indescribable blank in the text, a classic scapegoat whose
stammer is a symptom of the psychopathology aboard the *Bellipotent* and
at large in the postbellum state. He is a peacemaker, his speech a bearer of
unambiguous meanings. His occasional imperfect speech signals mental
gaps, lapses in cognition that have subversive potential and tragic consequences. In Melville's tale, this vocal defectiveness (read psychic fragility) is
swiftly brought under control and recycled to good use by Captain Vere.
In the final scene, Billy's linguistic nervousness takes the form of an electric eloquence, which mesmerizes the masses to utter unwilling assent to the
oppressing classes:

> Without volition, as it were, as if indeed the ship's populace were but
> the vehicles of some vocal current electric, with one voice aloud and
> aloft came a resonant sympathetic echo: "God bless Captain Vere!" And
> yet at that instant Billy alone must have been in their hearts, even as in
> their eyes. (123)

Billy's stuttering is the performative at work in the language system,[1]
which brings to light more insidious forms of linguistic disease. Claggart is

two-faced and double-voiced: his words, psychotically estranged from their intent, signify mental disturbance. To heighten this impression of "something defective or abnormal in the constitution and blood" (67), Melville has him speak with the hint of an alien accent. Captain Vere's language problems are harder to diagnose. On the surface he would seem to embody the ideal rhetoric and political correctness of Melville's post-Civil War America. Vere's speech is a direct, powerful, and effective political rhetoric: Vere has the power to unify conflicting communities of speech. However, the alacrity with which he tries Billy by a "drumhead" court, instead of consulting the admiral, and his inflamed appeal to the court to consider only the blow's consequences, not the effective chain that caused it, suggest a chaotic system of reasoning. The inarticulate, degenerate speech of the masses and the disarticulated voice of political authority share an uncanny spectrum: "Who in the rainbow can draw the line where the violet tint ends and the orange tint begins? . . . So with sanity and insanity" (*Billy Budd* 102).

In *Billy Budd,* the instability of the spoken word threatens to induce an anarchic state. Gilles Deleuze celebrates this kind of literature, which imaginatively uses linguistic vagary to signal political upheaval, and wherein stuttering occurs beyond speech, in language itself:

> It is no longer the character who stutters in speech; it is the writer who becomes *a stutterer in language*. He makes the language as such stutter: an affective and intensive language, and no longer an affectation of the one who speaks. [. . .] This is the principle of a poetic comprehension of language itself; it is as if the language were stretched along an abstract and indefinitely varied line. ("He Stuttered," 107–109)

The stuttering that sets a language system in motion is not merely a matter of inserting dialogic markers or modulations (he murmured, stumbled, coughed, faltered, quavered, etc) or making the characters murmur, stumble, cough, falter or quaver. It is "creative stuttering," says Deleuze, which makes language an immanent process of creation, a process that operates in the middle (*au milieu*), and proceeds by "series" or "plateaus" to new connections: "Creative stuttering is what makes language grow from the middle, like grass; it is what makes language a rhizome instead of a tree, what puts language in perpetual disequilibrium" ("He Stuttered" 111). This Deleuzian perception of stuttering, which considers the symptomatic stutter not as a "*form of expression*" but with a corresponding "*form of content*" ("He Stuttered," 108), is a useful heuristic for exploring the connection between hysteria and trauma in Pat Barker's *Regeneration* trilogy.

In *Studies on Hysteria* Freud regards hysterical symptoms "as the effects and residues of excitations which have acted upon the nervous system as traumas" (146). Traces are left behind because "abreaction" or thought-activity has not discharged the original excitation, and that psychical excitation is converted in hysteria into chronic somatic symptoms. Freud's history of Emmy von N., one of the five case studies that comprise *Studies on Hysteria,* looks at traumatogenic stuttering as a hysterical symptom. This is Freud's first case in which he used Breuer's method of catharsis, and contains in germinal form such psychoanalytic fundamentals such as free association and the concept of cathexis. Emmy von N. is a forty-year-old widow whose hysteric *tic* is a stutter and intermittent clacking. Freud diagnoses both motor manifestations as speech-inhibition mechanisms that have been precipitated by the patient's terror of uttering a word or making a noise. A conflict has occurred between the patient's intention and the antithetic idea or counter-will and it is this impasse that has lent to the discontinuous character of the *tic.* The tonic spasms of stuttering testify to inhibition, while the breakthrough of involuntary sound (clacking) marks the failure of that self-induced prohibition. Both are attempts to block ideas that are opposite in nature to those which the conscious will aims to express. Frau von N. is every hysteric: a woman with a past (and a horde of pathological memories), her sexual desires are severely repressed and inextricable from disgust, and she nurses a grievance for patriarchal authority figures. Freud shows us the inherent connection between Frau Emmy's repressed and feared ideas (or wishes) from the past, and the feared events she describes as precipitating the stutter. The common anxiety is that a child may be harmed or killed. The stutter enacts a regression from speaking to eating, and testifies to a predominance of the painful antithetic idea of devouring and reincorporating the children. Words are not used literally or figuratively but have become obscenely intimate, all mouth: it is a return to the state of pre-ego and the semiotics of mother-child identity. Freud treats Emmy von N. with hypnotic psychotherapy, pitting her pathological fixations against opposing ideas, assurances, and prohibitions, and combating the premises on which the symptoms are erected. Therapeutic success, however, is short-lived. Freud attributes this failure to Frau von N.'s severe neuropathic heredity and her retention of large sums of excitation over many years, which remained inaccessible, and consequently unplumbed, by her doctor. In a footnote appended to the case study in 1924, Freud writes: "I am aware that no analyst can read his case history today without a smile of pity" (167).

Vocalic deviation in Barker's novels, as embodied in the stutter, functions as a creative breach in knowledge and consciousness. In Barker's

Freudian rendition, the neurotic stutter is a speech act, which unintentionally does more than it says. It stands for the speaking body, and points to an incongruous and inseparable relationship between spirit and matter, discourse and act, the linguistic and the physical. The stutter is a symptom or diagnostic, an act that cannot know what it is doing, a vivid instantiation of a knowledge that cannot know itself. It is a reliving of trauma that defies and propagates its reality at once. In this chapter I hope to develop an analytics of the stutter and show in the course of my argument how the rupture of/in speech is understood at once as the traumatic symptom, a political performative (which mediates between memory and amnesia, conscious and unconscious "knowledge," lost and found identity), and the disruption that enables a narration of the nation.

I. "ALICE IN HYSTERIALAND"

Walking down a converted children's ward, the Cambridge neurologist and anthropologist Dr. W. H. R. Rivers glances at copies of Tenniel's drawings from *Alice in Wonderland* and contemplates their relevance in a military facility for the psychological casualties of the Great War: "All those bodily transformations causing all those problems. *But they solved them too.* Alice in Hysterialand." (*The Ghost Road* 24). When, in September 1914—a month after the war had broken out—the first cases of men suffering from some sort of a nervous breakdown began to arrive back in Britain, the War Office and medical establishment were forced to consider the connections between the horrors of warfare and the hysterical symptoms of an increasing group of paralyzed, benumbed, and dumbstruck men. Though Freudian theories about the psychogenesis of hysterical symptoms were applied to soldiers suffering shellshock with no apparent organic basis, the term hysteria—always associated with women of infirm constitution—was not applied unequivocally to the different forms of war neurosis. Doctors tended to use it only in reference to the lower ranks, while labeling the chiefs of staff "neurasthenic." This nervousness about using "hysteria" and "trauma" as the names for interchangeable or even inter-implicated disorders is still prevalent, and can help explain the wide cultural circulation of Post-traumatic Stress Disorder (PTSD) while hysteria disappears from the psychoanalytic account.

"Hysteria may need its trauma, but does trauma produce hysteria?" asks Juliet Mitchell (180). Hysterics and trauma victims suffer alike from "reminiscences": according to Mitchell, in both cases, memory has regressed to a fixed perception, a distorted iconic presentation of the traumatic shock.

> At the very moment of trauma there is neither perception nor memory.
> Something experienced as traumatic shock eradicates the victim's capac-
> ity for memory as representation. In its place comes the perception, the
> presentation of the experience. [. . .] The trauma victim and the hys-
> teric are akin (or are sometimes one and the same person) because they
> cannot remember, they can only perceive. (281)

Though he abandoned the "neurotica" of seduction theory in 1897, Freud
maintained that trauma, actual *or imagined,* was the cause of hysteria. Hysterics suffered from gaps in memory caused by repression. The difference
between normal forgetting and hysterical-pathological amnesia is that repression occurs in response to a psychic trauma in the latter. Psychic trauma
breaks through the subject's protective cortical shield: hysterical repression
is an unconscious mode of dealing with this breach in the mental apparatus
and the flood of excitation that threatens it. The repressed material, however,
returns, not as a memory (which was repressed) but as the raw perception
of event itself: the hysteric suffers from the compulsion to repeat traumatic
experiences. To go back to Mitchell's distinction between memory and perception, the hysteric does not remember—there is nothing to remember—
but perceives new, displaced images of a past which comes to being in the
present. While memory is a safeguard, something that gives content and
context to the past by forcing a plot on a mass of traces, perception chains
the hysterical and traumatized alike to an overabundant, undifferentiated,
and atemporal consciousness.

   Freud compares war trauma to hysterical neuroses in *Beyond the Plea-*
sure Principle, thereby suggesting that it involves an internal, as well as an
external stimulus:

> [Perceptual unpleasure] may be perception of pressure by unsatisfied
> instincts; or it may be external perception which is either distressing in
> itself or which excites unpleasurable expectations in the mental appara-
> tus—that is, which is recognized by it as a "danger." (11)

The victim of trauma, according to Freud, is threatened both from the
inside and the outside. In other words, trauma is not merely a response to
an external shock: as with hysteria, its perceptual unpleasure results from
ego conflict, whether induced by repressed wishes or an external perception.
Trauma and hysteria also have in common a destructive element: the death
drive. The shellshock victim repeats the perception of the traumatic experience so as to bind the excitations and integrate the event in his psychic life.

Yet, as Kaja Silverman states in her discussion of male subjectivity in the context of historical trauma, "the repetition through which psychic mastery is established exists in [. . .] an intimate relation with the repetition through which it is jeopardized" (61). The attempt at synthesizing traumatic material with normal mental processes degenerates inevitably into the compulsion to repeat trauma.

In repeating experiences that were unpleasurable neurotic subjects were therefore under the sway of something *beyond* the pleasure principle, and Freud placed this *beyond* in the biological infrastructure of the death drive. In "Introduction to *Psycho-Analysis and the War Neuroses*," Freud categorizes war neurosis as that in which the subject eschews the pleasure principle to succumb to the dissolution of his identity or ego. Freud's example of his grandson's *fort-da* game can be evoked as an illustration. Freud interpreted this use of the signifier to represent presence and absence as a cultural achievement, and an entry into the symbolic domain. We have here a traumatized consciousness that had taken cognizance of a profoundly unpleasurable lack—the absence of the mother—and had then acted, by means repetitive play, to assume a tenuous form of mastery. However, repetition replicates the originary distress, and mastery is predicated on self-loss and a masochistic surrender to the order of language. As Lacan comments on the young subject's game of fort/da with the small bobbin, "the function of the exercise with this object refers to an alienation, and not to some supposed mastery, which is difficult to imagine being increased in an endless repetition" (*Four Fundamental Concepts* 239). In Lacan's supplementation of Freud's theory of unpleasurable repetition and the death drive, the beyond of the pleasure principle is the signifying chain, rather than the primordial masochism of the death drive. Lacan superimposes the Symbolic order, organized around a barred signifier, on Freud's energetic model of the death-drive, to delineate the battleground where identity is formed *and* most severely jeopardized.

Within weeks of beginning, the nature of the war had changed: in "method, style, character, spirit, aim, size," as Marc Ferro puts it (53). The nerve-damaging propensities of the war machinery—aeroplanes, tanks, gas, rapid-firing heavy caliber artillery, immensely heavy shell, and high-velocity steel-jacketed bullets—were largely unforeseen by medical and military personnel. According to Wendy Holden, as war impended a doctor in the *British Medical Journal* advocated alcohol as an instant cure for any psychological problems, while an officer of the 29th division claimed that the cure for fear was a minute tied to the barbed wire at the front. (11) "Home by Christmas!" warbled young foot soldiers in 1914, but with the failure of early British attempts to turn the German flank, the hopes of a short and victorious war faded. After the retreat at Mons and the first battle of the Marne in autumn 1914, millions of soldiers found themselves immobilized in water-filled trenches. The British were unprepared for a sustained conflict, outnumbered and outmaneuvered. Burying themselves in order to live, trapped in chalk-mud and surrounded by decomposing bodies of their dead compatriots, the men on the western front faced only one certainty: death for one or all. Captain Herbert Leland, of the 3rd (Reserve) Battalion South Straffordshire Regiment, wrote to his wife from the trenches: "I have not been feeling too well lately . . . How I do wish I could tell you some things. I dare not, of course, for you would never get my letters . . . I am absolutely deaf and as weary as a kitten" (*Shell Shock* 21) British forces suffered heavy casualties in Belgium and France. With an average of four hours' rest per day, and continual awareness of being within the range of German guns, the Allies waited in the trenches under orders from the brigade to hold on, not to retreat, to be killed rather than retreat. Gripped with this horror, men who had shown no previous signs of innate or hereditary mental illness lost a private war between sanity and madness.[2]

Psychiatry, as defined by the work of Sigmund Freud, Carl Jung, and Alfred Adler, was still a marginalized discourse: the London society for Psychoanalysis, set up in 1913, had attracted only a dozen members. The invisible injury of the First World War played a significant part in entrenching the categories, tenets, and techniques of English psychiatric practice, driving it to convert symptom into spoken word. Faced with a panoply of hysterical and neurasthenic disorders—paralysis, mutism, blindness, among regular soldiers, and nightmares, insomnia, dizziness, and depression, among officers—analysts debated over the most efficacious therapeutic approach. While one group valorized the catharsis of suppressed emotions leading to a resynthesis of mind, another emphasized the recall of the repressed scene, and a conscious reintegration of the dissociated memory into the patient's history.[3] The methodological difference entailed varying degrees of participation of the subject in the curative process, but both solicited a participatory, rather than coercive model of treatment. The symptom was recognized as a gestalt of motives and experiences that were necessarily out of the cognitive reach of the patient, and the general purpose of analytic treatment was to enable self-knowledge, and create a consistent end story. As Eric Leed says, the therapist functioned not as a protagonist "but as an 'operator' of a patient who was his own oracle."[4]

The overwhelming numbers of psychic disorders in this war—by 1916, forty percent of casualties in the fighting zones were "shell-shock cases" (Showalter, *The Female Malady* 168)—forced the authorities to categorize neurosis as acceptable behavior among combatants, but only after the medical establishment had judged the legitimacy of their claims, and attempted to exact a quick recapitulation and return. As Eric Leed states,

> Here the exit from war was policed and administrated. Within the drama of therapy the traditional "offensive" soldierly role was clarified and fitted upon those who desperately wished to repudiate it. At worst, the therapies administered to those made neurotic in war were acts of pure domination; at best, it was the scene of negotiations between the demands of authority and the needs of the victims of war. (165)

The reinstatement of the patient to the role he abdicated was accomplished through two antagonistic conceptions of treatment: disciplinary and analytic. Disciplinary therapists sought to make the consequences of the symptom acutely painful for the patient, who was then persuaded of its detrimental nature, and the absurdity of "maintaining" it. They used the electric-shock method to test the fixity of the symptom, and the power of personality in autosuggestion advocated by the German psychiatrist Dr. Fritz Kauffman. Disciplinary therapists like the Canadian-born Lewis Yealland were sent the most stubborn cases of hysteria, and succeeded in emphasizing the demands of public duty over the defensive ruses of ignominious private survival. The analytic treatment—most commonly represented by psychoanalysis—evolved as a reaction against the inhumanity of the disciplinary method. While disciplinary therapy treated the symptom as an expression of the will of the patient, the analysts asserted that it was wholly determined by unconscious motives and conflicts, which were then coerced into representation. Instead of imputing blame, the analytic method regarded the neurotic soldier as one who was helplessly divided between his instinct for survival and the social and moral imperatives that forced him to repeatedly risk his life. It sought to frame the reality behind the symptom in the traumatic reality of the war, and shared the responsibilities and costs of warfare.

The project of symbolizing war trauma, however, was severely marred by the intractability of the traumatic experience. Trauma persists necessarily as a failed or missed telos, dissolving itself as soon as we try to grasp its positive nature. It is never present to the subject in the form of affective representations that could be systematically retrieved. According to Ruth Leys, "trauma cannot be lifted from the unconscious because that trauma has never been "in" the unconscious in the form of repressed representations" (646). Devoid of the symptomatology of repression, the enigmatic core of trauma lies in its inherent latency: a beguiling misalignment between seeing an event and knowing it, immediacy and the form of belatedness it assumes. Its constitutive void preserves the ur-event of trauma in its literality; as Cathy Caruth states, the history of trauma "is referential precisely to the extent that it is not fully perceived as it occurs," a history that can be grasped "only in the very inaccessibility of its occurrence" (*Trauma: Explorations in Memory*, 8). The event is not assimilated at the time, but only belatedly, through constant iteration. One bears tortured witness to trauma retroactively. As Siegfried Sassoon wrote in an open letter denouncing the war:

> Shell shock: a delayed effect of horrible memory you can't forget. How many a brief bombardment had its long-delayed after-effect in the minds of their survivors, many of whom had looked at their companions and laughed while inferno did its best to destroy them. Not then was their evil hour, but now; now in the sweating suffocation of the nightmare, in paralysis of limbs, in the stammering of dislocated speech. (*Shell Shock* 24)

Psychoanalysis, as Peter Buse rightly observes, seeks to trace and explain present actions "in terms of a past which occupies the prime position of causality."[5] However, it exceeds the simple determinism of this model in its theorization of trauma, where it analyzes the deferred effects of a past cause uncertainly and tentatively. The past that was never fully experienced as it occurred makes the possibility of knowing or curing trauma intensely problematic. Greenberg and van der Kolk formulate the paradoxical form of flashback that constitutes trauma: "failures of recall can paradoxically coexist with the opposite: intruding memories and unbidden repetitive images of traumatic events" (191). The past, incomprehensible yet insistent, and imagistic, requires integration for the sake of a cure. Pierre Janet, the Salpêtrière psychologist, developed a complex formulation about the transformation of trauma. Distinguishing "traumatic memory" (that which inflexibly, unconsciously repeats the past) from ordinary or "narrative memory" (which Janet described as "the action of telling a story,"[6] that codes the past as *past*), Janet emphasized that the goal of therapy was to convert traumatic memory into narrative memory. Strictly speaking, there is no such thing as "traumatic memory," since memory is necessarily narratable and continuous. Janet uses the concept "only for convenience" (Leys, 655) to denote an aberration of memory whereby one is unable to assume a critical distance from present experiences, organize those experiences in their proper time and place, and communicate them in a linear narrative: as a patient of war neurosis wonders in *Regeneration*, "'things are real, you've got to face them, but how *can* I face them when I don't know what they are?"[7] The subject is often incapable of making with regard to the event the symbolic gesture of remembering, and thus he remains confronted by a difficult situation in which he has not been able to play a satisfactory part, one to which his adaptation had been imperfect. Janet's advocacy of mnemonic reconstruction involves narration, "presentification," the *"action of telling a story"*: "The teller must not only know how to [narrate the event], but must also know how to associate the happening with the other events of his life" (Leys, 654). Traumatic memory is wordless and static—the ultimate goal is to convert it to narrative memory, or conjure up a story with words. This chapter uses these categories to read Pat Barker's *Regeneration* trilogy as an allegory of the failure of the narrative project, which is at the same time, paradoxically, its great success.

II. TRAUMATIC MEMORY

In his essay, "Commitment," Theodor Adorno talks about "the resistance of great autonomous art to consumption" (*Notes to Literature II* 92). While the aesthetic effects of the work provide a lure to enjoyment, they also bar interpretation and incorporation, forming a catch in the throat, a *globus hystericus*[8] as it were:

> For while the moment of pleasure always recurs in the work's effect even if it has been extirpated from it, the principle that governs autonomous works of art is not effect but their inherent structure. They are knowledge in the form of a nonconceptual object. (Adorno, 92)

Adorno's praise for an inassimilable, autonomous art that, through its own self-estrangement, "rattles the cage of meaning" (78), is applicable to Pat Barker's *Regeneration* triptych. These novels of war neurosis and the regeneration of nerves come close to risking their provisional systemacity by internalizing the very threat to symbolization. The language play is structured around the "nonconceptual" density of trauma, which remains as a necessary counterpoint, a real kernel which blocks the flow of symbolization and memory.[9] The most elegiacally imagined scene of all is No Man's Land, a traumatic place of failures, of no words, a "place of desolation so complete no imagination could have invented it" (RG 44). Through one of its pluralized mouths, the text offers "No theory" (RG 80) as the only possible theory of trauma: there is nothing to tell, and the pathological urge to tell, to precipitate a body and community for one's phantom voice.

Regeneration (henceforth cited as RG) is a powerful account of life at a military hospital in Edinburgh. The year is 1917, and Craiglockhart is home to the shell-shocked of the First World War, to Siegfried Sassoon, man of letters, soldier pacifist and conscientious objector, to Wilfred Owen, budding war poet, and to Dr. W. H. R. Rivers, the neurologist undergoing his own crisis as he attends shattered nerves.[10] Barker followed up *Regeneration* (1991) with *The Eye in the Door* (1993) and *The Ghost Road* (1995). The two sequels follow the characters of the first novel into the last year of the war; the focus of *The Eye in the Door* is on the character of Billy Prior and the deadlock between patriotism and pacifism, while *The Ghost Road* alternates a retrospective of Rivers's past as an anthropologist in Melanesia with the travails of Sassoon, Owen, and Prior in the war's present.

The therapeutic scene in Pat Barker's *Regeneration* trilogy is dominated by Dr. Rivers, a figure of "psychiatric modernism"[11] who sees trauma as the limit that is always missed, but also emphasizes the necessity of preparing oneself for yet another (missed) encounter. The Cambridge psychologist and anthropologist, serving as a therapist in the Craiglockhart Military Hospital near Edinburgh, relies on what he calls "autognosis" or self-understanding:[12] this involves the discussion of traumatic experiences, and reeducation, whereby the patient is prodded to utilize his newly acquired knowledge of himself, and to healthily expend morbidly directed energy. Rivers does not deny the validity of neurosis, but defies its persistence: referring to the emotional grounds of the anti-war position, he is of the opinion that while they should be ignored, they must not be allowed to dominate either. Rivers seems less concerned with the reality of the memory of the trauma, than with its subsistence in the present, and its bearing on future actions. As he tells his star patient, Second Lieutenant Siegfried Sassoon, he is not interested in etiology or primal causes but in the result, the end (or ends) of the curative process. We are told that Rivers's treatment sometimes consisted simply of encouraging the patient to abandon his futile attempt to forget, and advising him instead to spend some part of every day in active recall. Neither brooding on the experience, nor disavowing it.

Rivers acknowledges the aberrant and polysemic referentiality of trauma, and espouses a form of self-understanding that is less troubled by the imperative to retrieve and eventually liquidate traumatic "memory." He is committed to a project of analyzing and formalizing narratives whose fidelity to individual experience is no longer of central importance. In a particularly intense encounter with Prior, Rivers tries to perturb the logic of his resistance, signed sometimes as "'I DON'T REMEMBER'" (p. 41), and sealed at others as "'NO MORE WORDS'" (43):

> "If you feel you can't talk about France, would it help to talk about the nightmares?"

"*No.* I don't think talking *helps.* It just churns things up and makes them seem more real."

"But they are real."

. . . .

"I mean *you*'re more or less saying: things are real, you've got to face them, but how *can* I face them when I don't know what they are?"(RG 51)

The "real," though unsignifiable in language, can nevertheless be addressed only through language. The patient is not coerced into instantiating primordial personal truths, but is urged to acknowledge what he cannot readily know, to circumscribe the impossible. In that respect, Rivers's work may be said to prefigure the work of the Lacanian school of psychoanalysis, which takes into account the failure of memory in trauma and yet advocates the need for a structural version of psychoanalysis, conceived "as a discipline that on the one hand invests patient narratives with decisive significance but on the other hand maintains that those narratives are characteristically, perhaps inherently, discrepant with the (themselves often unknowable) 'facts' of the case" (Leys, 660).

Memory and invention, or contingency and art, are mutually destructive in the therapeutic narration of trauma. Billy Prior can make sense of the past only through a structuralizing self-splitting, whereby he presents fragments of his past as if they were absurd events in somebody else's life. Rivers tries to deny him hypnosis, for the recounting of memory in hypnosis leads to its excision, not integration. The symptom—amnesia, in Prior's case—is cured, but not the dissociative disorder that gave rise to it. According to Rivers, patients dealt with an unbearable experience by splitting it off from the rest of their consciousness, but this in turn affected their ability to deal with any kind of unpleasantness. The tendency to cordon off horrible experiences is reinforced by hypnosis, which cured the symptom—loss of memory, for example—but also made the underlying condition worse. Rivers tries to break down the detachment, to excavate the emotion, and against himself, the analysand "'dredge[s] up the horrors,'" remembers the deaths (RG 79). He urges Prior to look into his past, but denies him the calibrated distance and detachment from the objects of his vision. If Prior is the empowered possessor of the gaze, he is also, like the divided subject of Hitchcock's *Rear Window,* an immobilized witness who cannot but observe what goes on, and in dire need of therapy.

Rivers's painstaking efforts to reconstruct the events leading to the attack that sent Prior to Craiglockhart, are met with mutism, hostility, helplessness, and what he finally acknowledges as Prior's unmistakable depression. Prior claims to have no memory, even when the past turns repeatedly in standard issue battle nightmares: he offers "No theory" and no story (RG 80). Rivers finally decides to grant him hypnosis, and access to an event (that can be vouchsafed as traumatic) that preceded his breakdown. Prior retraces his first trench watch, when a deceptively domestic scenario—his mates Sawdon and Towers crouched over a small fire made out of shredded sandbags and candle ends, coaxing the flames, frying bacon and making tea—is snuffed out by the firing of a shell. Nauseous and shocked, he was shoveling soil, flesh, and bone off the trench when he found himself locking eyes with an eye:

> Delicately, like somebody selecting a particularly choice morsel from a plate, he put his thumb and forefinger down through the duckboards. His fingers touched the smooth surface and slid before they managed to get a hold. He got it out, transferred it to the palm of his hand, and held it out towards Logan. He could see his hand was shaking, but the shaking didn't seem to be anything to do with him. 'What am I supposed to do with this gob-stopper?' (RG 103)

The disembodied eye, uncannily seeing him see it, disrupts Prior's relationship to his own reference: the tremors didn't seem to have anything to do with him. Towers's eye in the palm of his hand is like a hole in reality, a lack, a look without vision that shatters all narcissistic integrity. It is a disfiguring excess that swamps the symbolic, a mouth-stopper that stifles words: a numbness spreads all over the lower half of his face. The analyst is challenged by the symbolism the unconscious masterfully deploy—'What am I supposed to do with this gob-stopper?'—and his task, in this case, is to help Prior recognize, contextualize, and verbalize a single, disjunctive moment that holds its tongue, or fails to designate itself. Rivers resituates this episode as the apogee of the weeks and months of stress in a situation where from which there is no bolt-hole of escape and concludes, superego-like, that Prior did his duty and is thus above reproach. "'You even finished cleaning the trench" (RG 105). While Prior undermines the seriousness of what apparently robbed him of memory—"'It was *nothing*'" (RG 104)—Rivers strains to show through the hypnotic recall that it was in its spectrality, its lack of any correlatives in consciousness, that the traumatic event was experienced at all.

Prior's traumatic perception is repeated in *The Eye in the Door* (cited as ED). He is in Aylesbury Prison on a Ministry of Munitions errand, and has already sensed an uncanny familiarity with the place: "It was like the trenches. No Man's Land seen through a periscope, an apparently empty landscape which in fact held thousands of men" (ED 30). He experiences a flashback when confronted with a crude surveillance device, a painted eye on the cell door:

> The peephole formed the pupil, but around this someone had taken the time and trouble to paint a veined iris, an eyewhite, eyelashes and a lid. This eye, where no eye should have been, was deeply disturbing to Prior. For a moment he was back in France, looking at Tower's eyeball in the palm of his hand. (ED 36)

He comes eyeball-to-eyeball in nightmares too, as he reports to Rivers in a therapy session:

> "I was was walking along a path in a kind of desert and straight ahead of me was an eyeball. . . . Huge. And Alive. And it was directly in front of me and I knew this time it was going to get me." He smiled. "Do whatever it is eyeballs do." (ED 133)

The non-symbolized returns in the guise of a traumatic object: the detached eyeball is a materialization of the unspeakable. Prior goes through a hysterical self-splitting in the course of the narrative; his dissociated self is controlled by drives and fantasy, and he becomes a "headless subject," Lacan's *sujet acéphal*, for the duration of a series of fugue-states. "'I was born two years ago. In a shell-hole in France. I have no father,'" tells the *other* Prior to Rivers before the onset of a violent paroxysm.

In Barker's novels, Billy Prior is figured as the in-between or the repressed of social, cultural, and sexual categories. Neither fish nor fowl, as his father said of him, Prior revels in transgression. He is a "seminal spittoon"(ED 11), sticking warring nations, classes, and gender roles up his arse, figuratively speaking:

> [. . .] on the other side of that tight French sphincter, German spunk. Not literally—they left a bit longer ago than *that*—but *there* nevertheless, the shadowy figures one used to glimpse through periscopes in the trenches, and my tongue reaching out for them. I thought,
>> Oh ye millions I embrace you,
>> This kiss is for the whole world . . . (GR 248)

In his private world and dangerous sexual acts, death and eros are interchangeable: nightmares always end as wet dreams. Prior's schizophrenic double appears as a vanishing mediator, and signals the impossibility and urgent necessity of a rational intervention between antithetical roles and identifications. Rivers delves into Prior's past to establish a continuum between earlier attacks and those ostensibly brought on by the war. Prior's incapacitating symptom, according to Rivers, may well have started as an unconscious strategy for dealing with unpleasant, conflictual situations: "'I think you found out how to put yourself into a kind of trance. [. . .] And then in France, under that *intolerable* pressure, you rediscovered it'"(ED 248). Rivers counsels an acceptance and understanding of this psychotic division, a momentary recognition of one's specular double: " 'There has to be a moment when you look in the mirror and say, yes, this too is myself.'" (ED 249).

In Sassoon's case—which, in Rivers's opinion, is more an anti-war complex than a war neurosis—Rivers redefines the traditional goals of a trauma cure, for Sassoon's attitude to his war experience is the opposite of what the therapist normally encountered. With Sassoon, the task is not simply the construction of a consistent case history, but a reinstatement of his patient to the rationale of war. *Regeneration* opens with Rivers reading Sassoon's argument against war, as contained in his letter to his commanding officer, titled "Finished with the War, *A Soldier's Declaration*." In this letter, Sassoon questions his duty to his country, if that duty must come at the expense of individual freedom and his duty to fellow citizens dying and suffering in vast numbers each day. Faced with the implacable logic of Sassoon's pacifism, Rivers questions the justifiability of the protracted war. The clarity and sanity of Sassoon's ideology unsettles him momentarily—it was as if he wanted Sassoon to be really ill.

Since Sassoon suffers from none of the nervous disorders displayed by other patients at Craiglockhart, Rivers embarks on a therapeutic process that makes his patient *re*consider the war memories and emotions that he remembered with extraordinary clarity and passion. Sassoon's Declaration and poetry, Rivers admits, are themselves hypersigns, manifesting a sublimatory hold over a dark period of nightmares and hallucinations. Rivers's technique involves not an alleviation but an intensification of Sassoon's fears and misgivings about his ideology and the war, so that the implosive potential of affect permits effective action: it was Rivers's conviction that those who had learned to know themselves in relation to excessive, traumatic accidents, and to accept their emotions, were less likely to be deranged by them.

What this process of "regeneration" unwittingly does, however, is cause the repeated suffering of the event without necessarily allowing for the recuperative departures from the site of trauma.[13] When Rivers meets Dr. Yealland, a fellow physician dealing with the psychoneuroses of war through disciplinary therapy, he is overwhelmed by the ideological similarities in their methodologically converse practices. Yealland's implacable injunction to his patient(s), "'*You must speak, but I shall not listen to anything you have to say*'" (231), implies a listening for the event, but not the survivor's forcible break from it. Barker's text allows us to understand Rivers's compounding unease in Yealland's presence through yet another disconcerting identification he is forced to make—Rivers's father, a speech therapist, too, had paid more attention to the form of his stammering son's speech than its content. It is in Yealland's electrical room that Rivers's function of assisting a discursive interpellation of trauma—and the violence implicit in that statutory gesture—is mimicked in "a grotesque parody of Adam naming created things" (235).

During the treatment that Yealland invites Rivers to witness, he locks himself, his patient Callan, as well as Rivers in, for there is no way out except following full recovery. Electric current is applied systematically to Callan's neck and throat, and Rivers, one with Callan in horror and empathy, traverses the immanent progression from pain, exhaustion, rebellion, and despair, to the return of "'the proper voice'" (233). Rivers is divided against his will in this nightmarish experience, and is both the executed—"He was himself very tense; all the worst memories of his stammer came crowding into his mind" (231)—and the executioner, institutionalized with Yealland in the business of controlling people. His remorse intensifies in a nightmare where he is treating a patient through what seems "uncomfortably like an oral rape" (236).[14] The dream patient is a composite figure of Callan and Prior, or Callan-Prior-Rivers-Sassoon, (the ghost-cry from the patient is the cry issuing from Rivers which finally truncates the dream), and Rivers can no longer deny his complicity in Yealland's project:

> On the face of it he seemed to be congratulating himself on dealing with patients more humanely than Yealland, but then why the mood of self-accusation? In the dream he stood in Yealland's place. The dream seemed to be saying, in dream language, don't flatter yourself. There *is* no distinction. (RG 237–38)

While Yealland cured the grosser maladies of the men, he, in an infinitely more gentle way cured verbal blockages and dysfluencies, psychosomatic disorders that were neither intentional nor entirely pathological, and that served to register the small, private protests of ineffectual men. The smart parting salutes of Sassoon and Callan, thus, seem like silent but terrible reproaches to Rivers, and are curiously interchangeable.

However, engaged though he is in the task of repressing the phantom articulations of the unconscious protest of his patients, Rivers helps

us conceive of the psychoanalytic space as not merely antagonistic and agonistic, but one of epistemological promiscuity, mutual seduction, mastery
and loss. He is as changed by their discussions as Sassoon is. He dreams
antiwar dreams, and stammers rather badly in Yealland's faradic laboratory:
Dispatching Sassoon to France, Rivers contemplates both on the extent of
his own influence and the irony that the patients have unwittingly radi-
calized and treated his own maladies: "'healing *does* go on, even if not in
the expected direction'" (RG 242). As a "male mother" (RG 107), he tri-
angulates with the binaries of patient-analyst, masculine-feminine, master-
slave, silence-speech, which cease to be inert substantives and contaminate
each other. The significance of this hypnoid identification can be explained
through Levi-Strauss's description of the ethnographic act: the ethnographic
object is constituted "by dint of the subject's capacity for indefinite self-
objectification (without ever quite abolishing itself as a subject) for pro-
jecting outside itself ever-diminishing fragments of itself."[15] The subject
becomes both subject and object in the process of charting its field of knowledge: the spectator is in fact the spectacle. Rivers's subjectivity too splits in
enunciation, becomes a self-focalizer, and views itself "in a courtroom where
he himself [is] both judge and jury" (p. 239). The interanimation of his
words, with *other*, ambiguous and grotesque signs—the stammer that cannot be cured, for instance—marks precisely the interpretable discontinuities
in the text, which are its truly historical moments,[16] and which are livid
with an inarticulable desire to *know* the nonmeaning, or true meaning of
the trauma of war.

III. NARRATIVE MEMORY

In Virginia Woolf's *Mrs Dalloway* "the shell-shocked veteran" is connected
with "the repressed woman of the man-governed world through their common enemy, the nerve specialist"; according to Elaine Showalter, Septimus
Smith, the victim of shell-shock in the novel, "perhaps owes something of
his name, his appearance, and his war experience to Sassoon" (*The Female
Malady*, 192). Septimus Smith came of age ("developed manliness")[17] in the
war, which he had joined in a usual muddle of "vanity, ambition, idealism,
passion, loneliness, courage, laziness" (MD, 84). He survives the death of his
friend and officer, Evans, and the last shells, and then the "panic was on him
. . . he could not feel" (MD, 86). Like Sassoon, he is gripped by an affliction beyond words, yet unlike him, Smith fails to negate his loss of being,
or mourn it through aesthetic representation. He is a figure of "cannibalistic
solitude,"[18] refusing to recuperate loss, or recount it, for fear of vitiating or

dispersing it: "now that he was quite alone, condemned, deserted, as those who are about to die are alone, there was a luxury in it, an isolation full of sublimity; a freedom which the attached can never know" (MD, 92). Like "some colossal figure who has lamented the fate of man for ages in the desert alone"(MD, 70) Septimus Smith mourns without feeling, memorializes the past without narrating it, remembers nothing, yet can forget nothing:

> "And you have a brilliant career before you," said Sir William. There was Mr. Brewer's letter on the table. "An exceptionally brilliant career."
> But if he confessed? If he communicated? Would they let him off then, his torturers?
> "I—I—" he stammered.
> But what was his crime? He could not remember it.
> "Yes?" Sir William encouraged him. (But it was growing late.)
> Love, trees, there is no crime—what was his message?
> He could not remember it.
> "I—I—" Septimus stammered. (MD, 98).

In the case of the fictional Sassoon of *Regeneration*, however, suffering tp quote Adorno, "demands the continued existence of the very art it forbids; hardly anywhere else does suffering still find its own voice, a consolation that does not immediately betray it" (*Notes to Literature II*, 88). For Sassoon, writing enables the requisite preservation of loss as a means of achieving liberation from it. It contains, in this respect, a fort/da motion that, as Madelon Sprengnether describes little Ernst's fort/da game, "institutionalizes both the act of renunciation and the impulse toward regression that inheres in it" (135). Sassoon writes as if his live depended on it and acts as literary gadfly with Wilfred Owen, convincing him finally that it's mad not to write about the war when it's "Such an *experience*" (RG 124–5). Owen stutters badly when he defends the idea of a transcendental poetics in a time of war:

> "I s-suppose I've always thought of p-poetry as the opposite of all that. The ugliness." Owen was struggling to articulate a point of view he was abandoning even as he spoke. "S-Something to to t-take refuge in." (RG 84–5)

While Sassoon is right to point out the escapism of this position, his own writing seems to precipitate deadlock and interminable analysis. Writing attenuates as well as renovates memory. It perpetuates memory in a bounded space, and, as Rivers recognizes, the process of transformation "consists almost entirely of decay" (184). Sassoon is dogged by hallucinations, leftovers of the symbolic that return untransubstantiated, and he is still utterly incapable to think about after the war. Sassoon's narrative memory is as much a self-presentation as it is an act of self-alienation. Through linguistic reprisal, he stages the trauma of his own disappearance. This necessitates a rethinking of Janet's project of "presentification": ostensible mastery is based upon radical loss, and endless, immobilizing repetition. Sassoon suffers from reminiscences—the recital of the past *as past* is also a reiteration of "a genuine and very deep desire for death" (250). The repetition through which mastery is obtained exists in a parasitic relation with the repetition through which it is jeopardized. As Iain Chambers states, "The utopic dream of eventual arrival (and the consolation of an intellectual, political and historical completion) now reveals a gap in which some of us begin to lose ourselves" (245).

Chambers proposes the idea of the 'stutter' as a critical tool to assess the uneven passage from the utopic to the heterotopic. Citing Foucault, he adumbrates that while utopias "run with the very grain of language . . . heterotopias . . . desiccate speech, stop words in their tracks, contest the very possibility of grammar at its source; they dissolve our myths and sterilize the lyricism of our sentences" (Chambers, 245). The metonymic excess in every stutter structures the logic of the self-same with something *else,* something *more,* and that aporetic void of unknowing becomes *stricto sensu* the absent cause—the regenerative lack—of the symbolic order, and a positive condition of our subjectivity (in language). The stutter is a "leaky habitat," wherein, as Chambers poetically formulates, "the violent transitivity of language [. . .] erupts most starkly across the hyphen of hybridity" (248).

The etiology of the stutter is highly controversial: a discrepancy between the thought tempo and the speech tempo, febrile illness, forcible conversion from left- to right-handedness, worrisome environment, physical or mental shock, hypercritical parents. "Don't tickle your child too much or he will stutter," the saying goes in deepest North Carolina, while being caught in the act of masturbation by a parent has reported links with the onset of stuttering. Neuroscience views the disorder as a physiological one as opposed to a psychological one. Recent issues of the *Brain* suggest that there are underlying differences in sensorimotor function in stuttering subjects. The right and left hemispheres of the brain play distinct and opposing roles in the generation of stuttering symptoms: activation of left hemispheric regions appears to be related to the production of stuttered speech, while activation of right hemispheric regions may represent compensatory processes associated with the attenuation of stuttering symptoms. The causes of this serious malfunctioning, however, still remain unknown. As Margaret Drabble, a stammerer herself, writes:

A stammer is not a physical disability, nor even a motor dysfunction, and that is that. All those cruel experiments with vocal cords and the slitting of tongues and the binding of left hands were a total waste of time. The nice elocution lessons I went to as a child in Sheffield were largely a waste of time, though I did learn some good poetry through them. The problem—and it is a problem, not a blessing in disguise, for most of us—remains a mystery.[19]

All stutterers are not neurotic; this chapter is particularly concerned with nervous stammers, and with dysfluencies that are caused, or activated, by traumatic impact. The neurotic stutter is a learned, self-defensive reaction to anxiety or fear of threatening circumstances with which the person feels incapable of coping. As Rivers says of other forms of traumatic neuroses, it is sometimes the "sole defence against the unbearable" (*The Ghost Road* 56). Contradicting the behaviorist view that a stutterer adopted the condition to avoid communicating, Joseph Sheehan, the famous speech pathologist, held that stuttering was a double approach-avoidance conflict with the stuttering repetitions and prolongations representing the precarious equilibrium between the drives to speak and to keep silent. Based upon primary traumatic experiences of failure in the performance of a learned skill or a simple motor or sensory act, often in socially embarrassing situations, the anticipation of this neurotic disturbance leads to a vicious spiral. What is most feared then becomes the object of a self-defeating repetition and desire. Like the infant who stages the *fort/da* game, staging the recall of the lost object only by making it disappear first, the stutterer achieves a non conflictual, if not happy, state by repeating the very perception he sought to circumvent.

Before the development of psychoanalytic explanations for stuttering, the condition was treated as a failure or weakness of the vocal apparatus, and could thus be remedied by strengthening the vocal apparatus. Early Freudian psychoanalysts saw stuttering as symptomatic of oral or anal fixations. To I. H. Coriat (1931), stuttering was the compromise symptom that partially solved the conflict between the instinctual need to remain an infantile suckling and the ego-need for more appropriate behavior. The patient, replacing consonants with clicks, was enjoying a powerful oral eroticism, though not without attendant anxiety. Fenichel (1945), on the other hand, argued that stuttering is a pregenital conversion neurosis in that the early problems dealing with the retention and expulsion of the feces have been displaced upwards into the sphincters of the mouth. For the stutterer, speaking affords an opportunity to smear and soil his listener aggressively, and with impunity; the concomitant panic felt by the stutterer is due to his unconscious realization of the symbolic nature of his symptoms.[20] Dated though these theories may be, they emphasize the unspeakable nature of the unspoken. The stutter dislocates voice, and throws into ontological uncertainty the body that it breaks away from. It commands a different spatial-sensory orientation, a seeing-hearing that will do justice to "an alternative store of memory in the nerve endings" (ED 272).

War, says Jacqueline Rose, "mimics or participates in the fundamental ambivalence of civilization itself. [. . .] The familiar destructiveness of war represents not, as is commonly supposed, finality but uncertainty, a hovering on the edge of what, like death, can never be totally known" (*Why War?* 16–17). The attendant alienation seems to stem from the fact that war is a free choice that turns out to be a forced one. War is an alien-ness in the very heart of identity or knowledge: to quote Rose again, "war is in some sense the repressed of its conceptualization" (24). Dr. Rivers gains a deeper understanding of the futility and necessity of the ongoing war during a delirious fever in *The Ghost Road,* when he returns in memory to his experience studying a South Pacific tribe. That was a people perishing from the absence of war, as evidenced in the decline in the birth rate. In a feverish moment of cross-cultural recognition, Rivers acknowledges a voluptuous death drive, and the need for immersion in the destructive moment. War advances civilization if only because it signals the death of certainty, and the dissolution of absolute knowledge that gave rise to it. According to Gertrude Stein, the suspended state of war—it is and it is not—deconstructs belief in evolution, or progress: "Certainly nobody no not anybody thinks that this war is a war to end war . . . they cannot take on the future, no really not, certainly not as warless certainly not as future."[21]

Rivers himself is deeply traumatized by the so-called Craiglockhart success stories: men who didn't remember, didn't feel, and didn't think, but whose nerves were steady (GR 200). These were battle servicemen whose minds were worn down with the struggle between conflicting instincts—the desire to run away and the obligation to stay—and whose symptoms had offered a bolt-hole of escape without capitulating to either side. "I survive out there by being two people, sometimes I even manage to be both of them in one evening," Sassoon had confessed (ED 229). Rivers despairs of having to cure splittings of personality engendered by the war: "Perhaps, contrary to what was usually supposed duality was the stable state; the attempt at integration, dangerous" (ED 235). The stammer marks the recalcitrance of the drive as that which cannot be totalized or included into the narrative frame, that which cannot be forgotten either since it repeats itself incessantly. The contingent traumatism of the stutter—"a conflict between wanting to speak and knowing that w-what you've got to say is not acceptable" (RG 97)—is no simple failure of language, but a refusal of failure, and an invitation to the other of the symbolic. Barbara Johnson calls the stutter a "deadly space" (83) within language, a discontinuity that makes the act of interpretation impossible. The epistemology of the stutter can also be conceptualized in the context of "DissemiNation," where Homi Bhabha talks about the "nation's interrupted address,"

> articulated in the tension signifying the people as an *a priori* historical presence, a pedagogical object; and the people constructed in the performance of narrative, its enunciatory 'present' marked in the repetition and pulsation of the national sign. (299)

The pedagogical draws its narrative authority from "a moment of becoming designated by *itself*, encapsulated in a succession of historical moments that represents an eternity produced by self-generation" (299). Bhabha cites the eccentric and stammering S. S. Sisodia from Salman Rushdie's *The Satanic Verses* and his litany of "what's wrong with the English": "The trouble with the English is that their history happened overseas, so they don't know what it means."[22] Bhabha agrees with Sisodia that history happens outside the center, necessarily and contingently. It is constituted and performed by the likes of S. S. Sisodia (whose name, in this form at least, itself graphically mimics a stutter), in non-recursive and heterogeneous forms of living, writing, and speaking. The performative disrupts the prefigurative self generation of the pedagogical, makes the other intrinsic to and disfiguring for the self-identical subject, and privileges the ontology of the "gap," the "in-between" over the infinite regression of binaries.

> The barred Nation *It/Self*, alienated from its eternal self-generation, becomes a liminal form of social representation, a space that is *internally* marked by cultural difference and the heterogeneous histories of contending peoples, antagonistic authorities, and tense cultural locations. (Bhabha, 299)

Pat Barker's novels participate in this performative hysterization—or dissemination—of the nation. Rivers is the most notably chiasmic figure in the novel, medicine's split-face negotiating the claims of humanity against the claims of a national war, doubly inscribed as a pedagogical object and a performative subject.[23] His report on military training for the Medical Research Council denounces the prolonged systematic repression of minds going through modern warfare, arguing instead to let the imagination play around the trials and dangers of warfare. Prior looks at his illegible and unfinished manuscript and calls it "the graphic equivalent of a stammer": "I mean, whatever it is you couldn't say, you certainly didn't intend to write it" (ED 257).

Diagnosing Sassoon's anti-war neurosis, Rivers tells him that it is his duty to try to change it and that he could not pretend to be neutral. In the process of assessing the genuineness of Sasoon's symptoms, however, Rivers faces the implacable imperative of questioning, interrupting, and deconstituting the validity of the demands of war. He cures the stammerings, the nightmares, the tremors, and the memory lapses without desublimating them in the psychoanalytic question: instead, the symptom is tropologically transferred from patient to analyst, and, as a catastrophic, psychosomatic double of discourse, signifies prosthetically "the sheer extent of the *mess*" (249). Rivers's *autognosis* reveals war neurosis—"'I already stammer and I'm starting to twitch'" (140).[24] As Prior, a formidable adversary on the couch, correctly diagnoses, Rivers's power over people, the power to heal, springs directly from some sort of wound in him. In helping his patients to know themselves, to abandon repression, and to let themselves feel the pity and terror their war experience inevitably evoked, he excavated his own moral ground. In the deserted corridor of a hospital, he allows himself a non-passive endurance of an impossible, phantasmagoric reality: "Uncanny. Almost the feeling his patients described, talking about their experience of the front, of No Man's Land, that landscape apparently devoid of life that actually contained millions of men" (223). Rivers realizes, as he did while conducting anthropological research in the Solomons, that once again, there is "'no measure'" (242), no way of assimilating and domesticating this experience; there are no commensurate signifiers. He encounters the immanent necessity of war instead with his own involuntary protest. The Proteus-like stammer revives and repeats a scene that cannot be designated in/as language: "If anything, he was amused by the irony of the situation, that he, who was in the business of changing people, should himself have been changed" (248–9). By internalizing the other, the lack that is also an excrescence, Rivers anthropomorphizes the liminality of the nation-space—the 'difference' is turned from the boundary 'outside' to its finitude 'within.' Janet's evolutionary optimism is dispersed in a narrative performance that both rearticulates and disarticulates the past as past: "the finitude of the nation," to quote Bhabha, "emphasizes the impossibility of such an expressive totality with its alliance between an immanent, plenitudinous present and the eternal visibility of a past" (302).

Iain Chambers writes poignantly of the human cost of deconstructing the past, its critical traditions and schools of thought: "We cannot go home again but neither can we simply cancel that past, or eradicate the desire for the myth of homecoming, from our sense of being and becoming." He insists that it is worthwhile to subsume loss in a "critical mourning," which opposes the "close teleology of identity and authenticity" with the disruptions that arise from the "radical historicity of language and existence" (249). A novel as obsessed with an individual's imaginary relationship with the symbolic as *Regeneration* teems with phantasmatic parricides. In Part III of *Regeneration* Rivers returns to his home parish for part of his leave, and confronts his old, cold anger at his own father. As a speech therapist and a priest, the father represents the combined disciplinary clout of state, school and church. At the age of twelve, Rivers had pulverized his authority by stuttering his way through a speech in support of Darwin's theories of evolution, forcing the patriarch to register the content of his words, not just his linguistic ineptitude. Rivers himself is used to being adopted as a father figure—at the receiving end of Prior's petulance and anger, he even identifies with his father—but Rivers also plots the most grievous injury to a cannibalizing father who is repulsive for being a constant frame of reference: "A society that devours its own young deserves no automatic or unquestioning allegiance. Perhaps the rebellion of the old might count for rather more than the rebellion of the young" (249). Sons will usurp the position of the father, the giant, and the empire-builder. Like HCE in James Joyce's *Finnegans Wake* Rivers stutters in anxiety as the Oedipal conflict comes to a head and braces himself for a "Phall" such as Finnegan's. He throws himself into his impossible task with a "critical mourning" that is also ours, for we cannot always cancel what we most passionately interrogate: "There was nothing more he wanted to say that he could say" (250).

Chapter Five
Emetic Theory: Conclusion

In Jonathan Franzen's *The Corrections* (2001), Chip Lambert, assistant professor of English (tenure track) in D—- College, has something of a professional identity crisis while teaching the intro theory course "Consuming Narratives" to first year undergraduates. A gifted female student makes him aware that he has been shoring the discontinuous fragments of contemporary critical and cultural theory to fabricate a positive ontology of his own. "This whole class," says Melissa Paquette accusingly, "It's just bullshit every week":

> It's always the death of this and the death of that. And people who think they're free aren't 'really' free. And people who think they're happy aren't 'really' happy. And it's impossible to radically critique society anymore, although what's so radically wrong with society that we need such a radical critique, nobody can say exactly. (44)

Chip is shaken to realize that he had taken his father's injunction to do work that was "useful" to society seriously enough, and that even as he was trying to theoretically infiltrate concepts of "usefulness," and rework status quo definitions of "useful work," he was heavily invested in an abstract utility to his cultural criticism. No, he did not think it was bullshit. The lameness of certain theories—"the myth of authorship; the resistant consumerism of transgressive sexual transactions that the college had hired him to teach"—sticks in his craw again when he tries later, self-loathingly, to deploy them to justify sex with the adolescent Melissa. He loses his job consequently, and hits rock bottom as philosophical theorist when his $4,000 and many kilos worth of Marxist texts fetch sixty-five quid in the second-hand market.

So where exactly does Chip's critical drive become a death drive? Despite the minor disadvantages of not being a queer or a subaltern, he had taught Theory of Feminism, had a hundred-percent voting record with the

Queer Bloc, and had routinely packed his syllabi with non-Western writers. Chip's demise as a theorist, Franzen suggests, has everything to do with the condition of theory, that top dollar discourse for asking salient, foundational questions, which fails, however, to provide answers. As Oscar Wilde said in "The Critic as Artist," "Thought is degraded by its constant association with practice" (275). The failure to authenticate, represent, ground, and provide a monothetic language, or a singular taxonomy, is also of course the greatest (negative) accomplishment of theory. Theory's is a purposive uselessness. Instead of linearity, multiple sites of narrative; in place of continuity, interruption; where there once dominated metaphysical notions of home and self, or self-at-home, what Levinas calls the violence of transitivity (the surplus of being), liminality, subalternity, migrancy, intersections, dialogue. Critical thought, says Iain Chambers, "is ultimately condemned to instability and movement, to be always on the margins of ironically subverting itself. . . . It exists as an act of interrogation: a moment of doubt, dispersal and dissemination" (*Migrancy, Culture, Identity* 121).

The title "Emetic Theory" uses a gustatory metaphor to delineate the object relations of theoretical judgment. In this usage, "emetic theory" doesn't mean "theory that disgusts and makes you sick" though it has been known to be seriously unpalatable to many. Nor is the disgust associated with vomiting here intellectualized to imply distaste or a sharp aesthetic distinction, which leads to an ejection of the offensive object in a paroxysm of revulsion. Emetic theory is theory as emetic: a methodology that does not involve eating, introjecting, or ingesting the object, or a gratification of appetite, but is instrumental instead in metaphorical purgation. Theory empties out transcendental categories, stopping metanarratives in their tracks, and affirmatively alienating identities and identifications.

Like Derrida, who poses disgust as inimical to the autotelic principles of aesthetics, Lacanian theory sees the symbolic as stained similarly by an obscene and intimate surplus existence: the real. The real, Lacan says in *The Four Fundamental Concepts,* is "the object that cannot be swallowed, as it were, which remains stuck in the gullet of the signifier" (270). The Real is impossible, a radical heterogeneity that threatens the life of the symbolic order. Lacan visualizes the order of the real as a *swarming* void, excess which is, however, virtual or not actual. The Real appears in the symbolic as the *objet petit a,* a lost object which sets in motion the vicissitudes of desire. There is, however, no question of incorporating the lost object in the unity of the selfsame. The real cannot be literalized or idealized—Lacan's and consequently Žižek's descriptions of it are in the mode of the paranoid Gothic—it threatens instead to swallow us up. Lacan describes our relation to the real not as a simple matter of recognizing or knowing it, but as an urgent responsibility, or what he describes as an ethical relation to the real. The real functions as an encounter, "insofar as it may be missed, insofar as it is essentially the missed encounter" (*Four Fundamental Concepts* 55). The missing of the real is also the only ethical encounter with the real.

Jean-Michel Rabaté aligns theory with Lacan's discourse of the hysteric. For the hysteric, object (a) is the truth—the hysteric's discourse engages with that preponderant, objectal "thingness" in the subject, which resists assimilation by language. The hysteric is a belligerent subject, forever questioning the mandate that locates her in the network of intersubjective relations. Žižek calls hysteria "the effect and testimony of a failed interpellation" (*Sublime Object*, 113), the failure of the subject to identify with the symbolic order. The hysteric's desire exceeds her demand, and her utterance falls short of her enunciation: to quote Žižek again, the hysteric position can be articulated as "'I'm demanding this of you, but what I'm really demanding of you is to refute my demand because this is not it!'" (*Sublime Object*, 112). The hysteric is after the phantasmatic surplus-object, the *objet a,* the real of *jouissance* which language has thrown up. Theory replicates this pattern of desire in that it too strains toward a traumatic impossibility, something that has to be addressed if not recuperated epistemologically. Joan Copjec calls the excess of the real "uncanny in the precise sense" because it is the inverse of the familiar: "It leeches familiarity from the familiar" (*Imagine There's No Woman* 97). Theory as emetic lets us glimpse at the contingent and constructed nature of its place and claims. It negates its at-homeness and homeliness from within. Whether in its expressive or vomitive capacity, theory hysterically rejects self-fulfillment.

Jean-Martin Charcot called hysteria "the great neurosis," one that could not be cured. In *Resistances of Psychoanalysis,* Derrida sees Freudian psychoanalysis as a new ethic of analysis that "began by analyzing a resistance" (16). In Derrida's account, Freudian analysis is not simply about exposing or uncovering the truth behind the symptom, but rather leading the patient to knowledge through effective and affective interventions that make the resistance intelligible, consequently unbinding and dissolving it. The greatest resistance Freud faced—Derrida calls it "absolute resistance" (23)—was not repression, but repetition compulsion, a resistance that has no meaning and cannot be worked through. And so it came to be that hysteria, with its incurable reminiscences and repetitions, constituted psychoanalysis as the analysis *par excellence* of resistances while simultaneously infecting and disorganizing that very principle. *Studies on Hysteria,* in its early and euphoric formulations of the process of recapitulation by which hysteria is cured, had already introduced the *pharmakon* of repetition, remedy turning to poison:

For we found, to our great surprise at first, that *each individual hysterical symptom immediately and permanently disappeared when we had succeeded in bringing clearly to light the memory of the event by which it was provoked and in arousing its accompanying affect.* . . . The psychical process which originally took place must be repeated as vividly as possible; it must be brought back to its *status nascendi* and then given verbal utterance. Where what we are dealing with are phenomena involving stimuli (spasms, neuralgias and hallucinations) these re-appear once again with the fullest intensity and then vanish for ever. (57)

Notes

NOTES TO CHAPTER ONE

1. As Ellmann says of her project in *The Hunger Artists:* "This book [. . .] is best described as a "phenomenology" in the sense that Gaston Bachelard has used the term, because its aim is not to find the cause of self-starvation but to follow the adventures of its metaphors" (15).
2. See Jacques Derrida, "Economimesis," trans. R. Klein *Diacritics* 11 (June 1981), 3–25.
3. See Ned Lukacher's foreword, "The Epistemology of Disgust," in *Hysteria from Freud to Lacan* vii-xxi.
4. See Jean-Michel Rabaté, *Jacques Lacan: Psychoanalysis and the Subject of Literature* (London: Palgrave, 2001) pp. 115–135 for an excellent discussion of the application of this psychoanalytic method to literary criticism. Rabaté focuses on Lacan's 1965 article on Marguerite Duras—his rhetorical homage to Duras—to argue that Lacan, playing the role of an analyst, wants to 'give back' to Duras her own text in an inverted form.

NOTES TO CHAPTER TWO

1. *Eastenders* is BBC's first soap, and one of UK's highest-rated programs, achieving some of the highest audiences in British TV history (30.15 million in 1986). Created in response to the realities of a post-1980s recession, it helped BBC receive its renewed 10-year charter in 1996. Set in a working-class neighborhood in the fictional borough of Walford in London's East End, it focuses on relationships of a mixed community of characters. Storylines often feature burning social issues like HIV, abortion, child abuse, domestic violence, and bullying.
2. Simon Shepherd and Peter Womack, *English Drama: A Cultural History* (Oxford: Blackwell Publishers, 1996), 239. Simon Shepherd is referring to the theatre anthropologist Eugenio Barba's distinction between performances

that aim to simulate daily reality, and those that defamiliarize it. If the "daily techniques" of the former category, have communication as its aim, the latter, according to Barba, uses "techniques of virtuosity" for "amazement and the transformation of the body" (*English Drama* 192).

3. *Nineteenth Century Plays,* ed. George Rowell (Oxford: Oxford University Press, 1992), 41. All references to *Black-Ey'd Susan, Lady Audley's Secret, Masks and Faces,* and *The Bells* are from this text and are cited parenthetically.

4. For a history of the Surrey Theatre see William G. Knight, *A Major London Minor: the Surrey Theatre 1805–1865* (London: The Society for Theatre Research, 1997).

5. See *English Plays of the Nineteenth Century. I. Dramas 1800–1850* ed. Michael R. Booth (Oxford: Clarendon Press, 1969), for the historical background of nautical melodrama.

6. See Barbara Charlesworth Gelpi, "The Politics of Androgyny," *Women's Studies* 2 (1974), 151–60. Gelpi talks about the utopian promise of wholeness which is, in actuality, another version of the male incorporation of the feminine.

7. *Times,* 29 May 1893, 8. The "old school" of critics, most prominently represented by Clement Scott, was apprehensive and dismissive of new developments in playwriting, the nature and extent of Ibsen's influence on British Drama, and the extent to which 'realism' was permissible on the stage.

8. In Lacanian theory, desire is structured by castration and the pleasure principle, while drive is not constrained by the energetics of the oedipal mechanism. If the ethics of desire is conducive for Eros and social life, the ethics of *jouissance* privileges Thanatos and the death drive. Desire is lawful and conscious, while drive, which implodes upon itself in enjoyment, is unlawful and unconscious.

9. Kaplan is citing Margot Peters here, author of *Mrs Pat: The Life of Mrs. Patrick Campbell.*

10. *Punch,* 10 June 1893, 273. See John Dawick, *Pinero: A Theatrical Life* (Colorado: UP of Colorado, 1993) 192.

NOTES TO CHAPTER THREE

1. See Forster's account of Dickens's plotting of *Great Expectations* in John Forster, *The Life of Charles Dickens,* 355–56.

2. See *The Dent Uniform Edition of Dickens' Journalism: The Uncommercial Traveller and Other Papers, 1859–1870* edited by Michael Slater and John Drew for Dickens's journalism around the time he wrote *Great Expectations.* Slater and Drew wonderfully bring out the two facets of Dickens's authorial persona: eminent Victorian, crusading for social reform, and a morbid fantasist, goaded in his literary pursuits by prurient curiosity and a wicked sense of humor.

3. Joseph A. Hynes identifies as the "Magwitch motif" the imagery of Pip's first encounter with Magwitch, which return in subsequent scenes. See "Imagery and Symbol in *Great Expectations,*" 290.

NOTES TO CHAPTER FOUR

1. Billy's utterance *performs* meanings, consciously or unconsciously. As performance-analysts points out, the speech act, or the act of a speaking body, obfuscates the distinction between body and language. The performative locution often seems unlinked to the subject, or the body that unknowingly participates in it, giving rise to alternative notions of agency and responsibility. Deleuze and Guattari, influenced by J. L. Austin, wrote in the *Thousand Plateaus* that language can be defined by "speech acts [doing by saying] current in a language at a given time" (79). See Shoshana Felman, *The Literary Speech Act: Don Juan with J. L. Austin, or Seduction in Two Languages* trans. Catherine Porter (Ithaca: Cornell UP, 1983), and Judith Butler, *Excitable Speech: A Politics of the Performative* for brilliant analyses of the relation between speech and action.

2. See "Shell Shock," Channel 4 series created by Blakeway Productions, and Wendy Holden's accompanying text of the same name.

3. For a detailed analysis of the medical therapeutics of psychoanalysis during World War I, see Ruth Leys, "Traumatic Cures: Shell Shock, Janet, and the Questions of Memory," *Critical Inquiry,* 20 (Summer 1994), pp. 623–62.

4. Eric J. Leed, *No Man's Land: Combat and Identity in World War I* (Cambridge: Cambridge University Press, 1979), p. 177. According to Leed, neurosis was functional for authorities because it provided a category of behavior that cast aspersions on the legitimacy of the war in the most ambiguous terms. Because of its muted moral and legal claims, neurosis was also seen as a compromise—and one ratified in the interests of the military establishment—that, unlike mutiny, both challenged the power of command through an individualized symptom, and evaded its disciplinary wrath.

5. Peter Buse, "Sinai snapshot: Freud, photography and the future perfect," *Textual Practice,* 10:1 (1996), pp. 123–145. Buse talks about the entanglement of the past and future in the present, as exemplified in Freud's reading of a frozen moment in "The Moses of Michelangelo."

6. See Leys for a thorough discussion of Janet's theories. See also Bessel A. van der Kolk and Onno van der Hart, "The Intrusive Past: The Flexibility of Memory and the Engraving of Trauma," in *Trauma: Explorations in Memory,* pp. 158–182.

7. Pat Barker, *Regeneration* (New York: Plume, 1993), p. 51. Future references will be cited parenthetically with the following abbreviations: Regeneration (RG), The Eye in the Door (ED), The Ghost Road (GR).

8. American nerve specialists of the 1860s and 70s, at pains to differentiate neurasthenia from hysteria, established interrupted speech as a hysterical

symptom. George Miller Beard wrote in *Practical Treatise on Nervous Exhaustion* that neurasthenia lacked an important symptom of hysteria: the feeling "as of a ball in the throat." Neurasthenics were prone to plentiful, if nervous, speech. See Beard, *A Practical Treatise on Nervous Exhaustion (Neurasthenia), Its Symptoms, Nature, Sequences, Treatment* (New York: E. B. Treat, 1888). See also Elaine Showalter, *The Female Malady: Women, Madness, and English Culture, 1830–1980* (New York: Penguin, 1985) pp. 121–144.

9. I am alluding to the Lacanian theory of the Real here, a palpable order of effects that persists in language and being although it lacks an imaginary-symbolic language consciousness. Lacan's thoughts on the Real occur frequently, but disjointedly in the first and second seminars, notably in "Introduction of the big Other" in Book II. Chapter 5 of *Four Fundamental Concepts of Psycho-Analysis* is helpful in its discussion of the impossibility of the real, and can be read alongside Trauma theory.

10. As Barker acknowledges in her "Author's Note" at the end of *Regeneration,* several characters were real people, celebrated in the fields of science and literature: Dr. W. H. R. Rivers, Dr. Lewis Yealland, Dr. Henry Head, Siegfried Sassoon, Wilfred Owen, and Robert Graves.

11. The third section of Showalter's *The Female Malady* is entitled "Psychiatric Modernism," and contains a chapter on shell shock and the work of Dr. W. H. R. Rivers. See pp. 167–95.

12. See Elaine Showalter, "Rivers and Sassoon: The Inscription of Male Gender Anxieties," *Behind the Lines: Gender and the Two World Wars* ed. Margaret Randolph Higonnet et al (New Haven and London: Yale University Press, 1987), p. 65. Showalter's article, precisely because of its psychobiographical nature, is an interesting foil to the narrativization of the Rivers-Sassoon encounter in *Regeneration.*

13. For a conceptualization of trauma as a necessary departure from the moment of its first occurrence, see Cathy Caruth, "Unclaimed Experience: Trauma and the Possibility of History," *Yale French Studies* 79 (1991), pp. 181–91.

14. Freud's dream of Irma's injection in his *Interpretation of Dreams* (1900–1901) is also one of "professional conscientiousness" (120). There too, an identity is articulated between Freud and his patient, Irma's traumatic sense of vulnerability mirroring Freud's knowledge of the fallibility of his analytic work.

15. Cited in Homi Bhabha, "Dissemination," *Nation and Narration* ed. Homi K. Bhabha (London and New York: Routledge, 1990), 301.

16. According to Cathy Caruth, the notion of trauma permits "*history* to arise where *immediate understanding* may not." This necessitates a rethinking of the referentiality of history, which, as Caruth argues, does not eliminate history, but repositions it in our understanding. The history of trauma is significant in its blankness. See "Unclaimed Experience," p. 182.

17. Virginia Woolf, *Mrs Dalloway* (New York and London: Harcourt Brace and Co., 1925), p. 86, hereafter cited parenthetically as MD.

18. Julia Kristeva, *Black Sun: Depression and Melancholia* trans. Leon S. Roudiez (New York: Columbia University Press, 1989), p. 71. According to Kristeva, the melancholic disavows negation of loss, or the therapeutic entry into the symbolic, and remains painfully riveted to the (lost) object. Kristeva describes the process as an "omnipotent devouring" whereby inexpressible mourning erects a tomb inside the subject.

19. Margaret Drabble, Last Public Lecture, Oxford English Faculty (Thursday October 18, 2001). For an insightful examination of the science and ethics of speech pathology, as embodied in Wendell Johnson's aptly nicknamed experiment, the "Monster Study," see Michael Erard, "Stutter, Memory," *Lingua Franca* (November 2001).

20. For a comprehensive medical history of stuttering, see Charles Van Riper, *The Nature of Stuttering* (New Jersey: Prentice-Hall, 1971). See also H. Freund, *Psychopathology and the Problems of Stuttering* (Illinois: Thomas, 1966), *Stuttering: A Symposium* (New York: Harper, 1958), H. H. Gregory, *Learning Theory and Stuttering Therapy* (Evanston: Northwestern UP, 1968).

21. Gertrude Stein, *Wars I Have Seen* (London: Batsford, 1945), p. 122. Cited in Rose, *Why War?*, p. 18.

22. Ibid., p. 317. I wonder why Bhabha edits Sisodia's utterance which, in Rushdie's text, unabashedly runs/stumbles as follows: 'The trouble with the Engenglish is that their hiss hiss history happened overseas, so they dodo don't know what it means.' *Satanic Verses* (Delaware: The Consortium Inc., 1992), p. 343.

23. Donald Pease sees the pedagogical and the performative as non-identical doubles that make "postnational narration" possible in two very different ways:

    The "pedagogical" subject who, in enunciating the preexisting statements of the national narrative, discovers in the state's act integrative of the nation an event for which there are no preconstituted categories with which to enunciate it, on the one hand, and on the other, the "performative" subject who, in enunciating postnational narrations that lack any preexisting place within the narrative order apart from the self-fading act of enunciating them as such, can only reiterate what the national narrative is always lacking.

    See Pease, "National Narratives, Postnational Narration," *Modern Fiction Studies* 43.1 (Spring 1997): 1–23.

24. In her last public lecture, Margaret Drabble wonders if bad faith, false position, or insincerity of intent activate and aggravate stuttering. She quotes John Updike's claim that "The paralysis of stuttering stems from the dead center of one's being, a deep doubt there."

Bibliography

Acker, Kathy. "A Conversation with Kathy Acker." With Ellen G. Friedman. *Review of Contemporary Fiction* 9.3 (1989): 12–22.

———. "A Few Notes on Two of My Books." *Review of Contemporary Fiction* 9.3 (1989): 31–36.

———. *Great Expectations*. New York: Grove Press, 1992.

Ackroyd, Peter. *Dickens*. London: Sinclair-Stevenson, 1990.

Adorno, Theodor W. *Aesthetic Theory*. Trans. Robert Hullot-Kentor. Ed. Gretel Adorno and Rolf Tiedemann. London: The Athlone Press, 1997.

———. *Minima Moralia: Reflections from Damaged Life*. Trans. E. F. N. Jephcott. London: New Left Books, 1974.

———. *Negative Dialectics*. Trans. E. B. Ashton. New York: Seabury Press, 1973.

———. *Notes to Literature Vol. II*. Trans. Shierry Weber Nicholsen. New York: Columbia UP, 1992.

———. *Prisms: Cultural Criticism and Society*. Trans. Samuel and Shierry Weber. London: Neville Spearman, 1967.

Archer, William. *Theatrical 'World' for 1893*. London: Walter Scott Ltd., 1893.

———. *Theatrical 'World' of 1896*. Walter Scott Ltd., 1897.

Armstrong, Isobel. "And Beauty? A dialogue: debating Adorno's *Aesthetic Theory*." *Textual Practice* 12.2 (1998). 269–89.

———. *The Radical Aesthetic*. Oxford: Blackwell Publishers, 2000.

Attridge, Derek. "Expecting the Unexpected in Coetzee's *Master of Petersburg* and Derrida's Recent Writings." *Applying to Derrida*. Ed. John Brannigan, Ruth Robbins and Julian Wolfreys. London: Macmillan, 1996. 21–40.

———. "Oppressive Silence: J. M. Coetzee's *Foe* and the Politics of the Canon." *Decolonizing Tradition: New Views of Twentieth-Century "British" Literary Canons*. Ed. Karen R. Lawrence. Urbana and Chicago: U of Illinois P, 1992. 212–38.

Barker, Pat. *The Eye in the Door*. London: Penguin, 1994.

———. *The Ghost Road*. New York: Plume, 1995.

———. *Regeneration*. New York: Plume, 1993.

Barnes, Julian. *England, England.* London: Picador, 1998.

Bataille, Georges. *Eroticism: Death and Sensuality.* San Francisco: City Lights' Publishers, 1986.

Baylis, Matthew, "The Real East Enders." *Evening Standard Magazine* (3/12/99). 33–34.

Bhabha, Homi K. "DissemiNation." *Nation and Narration.* Ed. Homi K. Bhabha. London: Routledge, 1990. 291–322.

Booth, Michael R., ed. *The Revels History of Drama in English Vol. VI 1750–1880.* London: Methuen, 1975.

Brooks, Peter, "Melodrama, Body, Revolution." *Melodrama: Stage Picture Screen.* Ed. Jacky Bratton et al. London: British Film Institute, 1994. 11–25.

———. *The Melodramatic Imagination.* New Haven and London: Yale UP, 1976.

———. *Reading for the Plot: Design and Intention in Narrative.* Cambridge, Massachusetts: Harvard UP, 1992.

Brain. 120.5 (1997).

Brain. Special issue of Stuttering 123.10 (2000).

Buse, Peter. "Sinai snapshot: Freud, photography, and the future perfect." *Textual Practice* 10.1 (1996). 123–45.

Cadava, Eduardo, ed. *Who Comes After the Subject?* New York: Routledge, 1991.

Carey, Peter. *Jack Maggs.* London: Faber and Faber, 1997.

Caruth, Cathy. "Introduction." *Trauma: Explorations in Memory.* Ed. Cathy Caruth. Baltimore and London: The Johns Hopkins UP, 1995.

———. "Traumatic Awakenings." *Performance and Performativity.* Ed. Andrew Parker and Eve Kosofsky Sedgwick. New York: Routledge, 1995. 89–108.

———. "Unclaimed Experience: Trauma and the Possibility of History." *Yale French Studies* 79 (1991). 181–91.

Chambers, Iain. "Leaky habitats and broken grammar." *Travellers' Tales: Narratives of Home and Displacement.* Ed. George Robertson et al. London: Routledge, 1994. 245–49.

———. *Migrancy, Culture, Identity.* NY: Routledge, 1994.

Clayton, Jay. *Charles Dickens in Cyberspace: The Afterlife of the Nineteenth Century in Postmodern Culture.* Oxford: OUP, 2003.

Coetzee, J. M. *Foe.* London: Penguin, 1987.

Copjec, Joan. *Imagine There's No Woman: Ethics and Sublimation.* Cambridge: The MIT Press, 2002.

Cornell, Druscilla. *The Philosophy of the Limit.* New York and London: Routledge, 1992.

Cox, Jeffrey N. "The Ideological Tack of Nautical Melodrama." *Melodrama: The Cultural Emergence of a Genre.* Ed. Michael Hays and Anastasia Nikolopoulou. New York: St. Martin's Press, 1996. 167–91.

Cuarón, Alfonso, dir. *Great Expectations.* Perf. Anne Bancroft, Ethan Hawke, Gwyneth Paltrow, and Robert de Niro. Twentieth-Century Fox, 1998.

David-Ménard, Monique. *Hysteria from Freud to Lacan: Body and Language in Psychoanalysis.* Trans. Catherine Porter. Ithaca: Cornell UP, 1989.

Dawick, John. *Pinero: A Theatrical Life.* Colorado: The University Press of Colorado, 1993.

Defoe, Daniel. *The Life and Adventures of Robinson Crusoe.* Ed. Angus Ross. London: Penguin, 1985.

Deleuze, Gilles. "He Stuttered." *Essays Critical and Clinical.* Trans. Daniel W. Smith and Michael A. Greco. New York: Verso, 1998. 1-7-14.

Deleuze, Gilles, and Felix Guattari. *Kafka: Toward a Minor Literature.* Trans. Dana Polan. Minneapolis: University of Minnesota Press, 1987.

Dent, Alan. *Mrs Patrick Campbell.* London: Museum Press, 1961.

Dews, Peter. *Logics of Disintegration: Post-Structuralist Thought and the Claims of Critical Theory.* London: Verso, 1987.

———. *The Limits of Disenchantment: Essays on Contemporary European Philosophy.* London: Verso, 1995.

Diamond, Elin. "Realism and Hysteria: Toward a Feminist Mimesis," *Discourse* 13.1 (1990–91). 59–92.

Dibdin, Thomas John. *Melodrame Mad! or, the Siege of Troy.* London: n. p., 1819.

Dickens, Charles. *Great Expectations.* Ed. Angus Calder. London: Penguin, 1985.

Derrida, Jacques. "Economimesis." Trans. R. Klein. *Diacritics* 11 (June 1981). 3–25.

———. *Resistances of Psychoanalysis.* Trans. Peggy Kamuf et al. Stanford: Stanford UP, 1998.

Drabble, Margaret. Last Public Lecture given to Oxford English Faculty on Thursday, October 18, 2001. *The Guardian* (19/10/01).

Duras, Marguerite. *The Ravishing of Lol Stein.* 1966. Trans. Richard Seaver. New York: Pantheon Books, 1986.

Eagleton, Terry. *The Ideology of the Aesthetic.* London: Blackwell, 1990.

The Economist (November 3rd-9th 2001).

Ellmann, Maud. *The Hunger Artists: Starving, Writing & Imprisonment.* London: Virago Press, 1993.

Feldstein, Richard, and Judith Roof, eds. *Feminism and Psychoanalysis.* Ithaca: Cornell UP, 1989.

Ferro, Marc. *The Great War 1914–1918.* Trans. Nicole Stone. London: Routledge Classics, 2002.

Fink, Bruce. *The Lacanian Subject: Between Language and Jouissance.* Princeton: Princeton UP, 1995.

Fitzgerald, Percy. *Principles of Comedy and Dramatic Effect.* London: n. p., 1870.

Forster, John. *The Life of Charles Dickens II.* New York: Charles Scribner's Sons, 1900.

Franzen, Jonathan. *The Corrections.* London: Harper Collins, 2001.

Freud, Sigmund. *Beyond the Pleasure Principle. The Standard Edition of the Complete Psychological Works of Sigmund Freud* Vol. 18. Ed. and trans. James Strachey. 24 vols. London: Hogarth, 1953–74.

———. "Charcot." SE 3. London: Hogarth Press, 1953–74.

————. *The Complete Letters of Sigmund Freud to Wilhelm Fliess.* Trans. and ed. Jeffrey Moussaieff Masson. Cambridge: Belknap Press of Harvard University, 1985.

————. *The Interpretation of Dreams* (1900). SE 4.

————. "Introduction to *Psycho-analysis and the War Neuroses*" (1919). SE17.

————. "Negation" (1925). SE 19.

————. *Studies on Hysteria.* SE 2.

————. *Three Essays on the Theory of Sexuality and Other Works* (1905). SE 7.

Fuss, Diana. *Identification Papers.* New York and London: Routledge, 1995.

Gelpi, Barbara Charlesworth. "The Politics of Androgyny." *Women's Studies* 2 (1974). 151–160.

Gilman, Sander L., Helen King, Roy Porter, George Rousseau, and Elaine Showalter. *Hysteria Beyond Freud.* Berkeley: U of California P, 1993.

Grayling, A. C. "The Last Word on Relativism." *Guardian* (2/6/01) Saturday Review, 8.

Greenberg, Mark S., and Bessel A. van der Kolk. "Retrieval and Integration of Traumatic Memories with the 'Painting Cure.'" *Psychological Trauma.* Ed. Bessel A. van der Kolk. Washington, D. C.: American Psychiatric Press, 1987.

Hadley, Elaine. *Melodramatic Tactics: Theatricalized Dissent in the English Marketplace, 1800–1885.* Stanford: Stanford UP, 1995.

Herman, Judith Lewis. *Trauma and Recovery.* New York: Norton, 1992.

Holden, Wendy. *Shell Shock.* London: Channel 4 Books, 1998.

Hynes, Joseph A. "Image and Symbol in *Great Expectations.*" *ELH* 30 (1963). 258–92.

Ibsen, Henrik. *Hedda Gabler.* Dover Publications Inc., 1990.

Jameson, Fredric. *The Political Unconscious: Narrative as a Socially Symbolic Act.* London: Routledge, 1989.

Jay, Martin. *The Dialectical Imagination.* Berkeley: U of California P, 1996.

Johnson, Barbara. "Melville's Fist: The Execution of *Billy Budd.*" *The Critical Difference: Essays in the Contemporary Rhetoric of Reading.* Baltimore: The Johns Hopkins UP, 1983. 79–109.

Jones, Gavin. *Strange Talk: The Politics of Dialect Literature in Gilded Age America.* Berkeley: U of California P, 1999.

Joyce, James. "Daniel Defoe." Trans. Joseph Prescott. *Buffalo Studies* 1 (1964). 7, 11–13, 22–35.

————. *Finnegans Wake.* London: Penguin Classics, 2000.

Kahane, Claire. *Passions of the Voice: Hysteria, Narrative, and the Figure of the Speaking Woman, 1850–1915.* Baltimore and London: The Johns Hopkins UP, 1995.

Kant, Immanuel. *Critique of Judgment.* Oxford: OUP, 1952.

Kaplan, Fred. *Dickens and Mesmerism.* Princeton: Princeton UP, 1975.

Kaplan, Joel H. "Pineroticism and the problem play: Mrs. Tanqueray, Mrs. Ebbsmith and Mrs. Pat." Ed. Richard Foulkes. *British Theatre in the 1890s. Essays on Drama and the Stage.* Cambridge: CUP, 1992. Pp. 38–58.

Kojève, Alexander. *Introduction to the Reading of Hegel: Lectures on the Phenomenology of the Spirit.* Ithaca: Cornell UP, 1980.

Kristeva, Julia. *Black Sun: Depression and Melancholia.* Trans. Leon S. Roudiez. New York: Columbia UP, 1992.

Lacan, Jacques. *Écrits: A Selection.* 1977. Trans. Alan Sheridan. London: Routledge, 1995.

———. *The Four Fundamental Concepts of Psychoanalysis.* 1978. Ed. Jacques-Alain Miller. Trans. Alan Sheridan. London: Penguin, 1994.

———. *The Seminar of Jacques Lacan, Book II: The Ego in Freud's Theory and in the Technique of Psychoanalysis,* 1954–1955. Trans. Sylvana Tomaselli. Cambridge: Cambridge UP, 1988.

———. *The Seminar of Jacques Lacan, Book III: The Psychoses.* 1955–1956. Trans. Russell Grigg. Ed. Jacques-Alain Miller. New York: Norton, 1993.

Leed, Eric J. *No Man's Land: Combat and Identity in World War I.* Cambridge: Cambridge UP, 1979.

Lyotard, Jean François. "Going Back to the Return." *The Languages of Joyce: Selected Papers From the 11ᵗʰ International James Joyce Symposium.* Ed. R. M. Bollettieri Bosinelli et al. Philadelphia: John Benjamin's Publishing Company, 1992. 193–210.

Leys, Ruth. "Traumatic Cures: Shell Shock, Janet, and the Questions of Memory." *Critical Inquiry* 20 (Summer 1994): 623–62.

Lund, T. W. M. " 'The Second Mrs. Tanqueray'; What? And Why?" Liverpool: Lee and Nightingale, 1894.

Lyotard, Jean François. "Going Back to the Return." *The Languages of Joyce: Selected Papers from the 11ᵗʰ International James Joyce Symposium, Venice 12–18 June 1988.* Ed. R. M. Bollettieri Bosinelli et al. Philadelphia: John Benjamins Publishing Company, 1992. 193–210.

McKeon, Michael. *The Origins of the English Novel 1600–1740.* Baltimore: The Johns Hopkins UP, 1987.

Meisel, Martin. "Scattered Chiaroscuro: Melodrama as a Matter of Seeing." *Melodrama: Stage Picture Screen.* Ed. Jacky Bratton et al. British Film Institute, 1994. 65–81.

———. "Speaking Pictures." *New York Literary Forum* 7 (1980). 51–67.

Melville, Herman. *Billy Budd, Sailor (An Inside Narrative).* Eds. Harrison Hayford and Merton M. Sealts. Chicago. U of Chicago P, 1962.

Miller, D. A. *Narrative and its Discontents: Problems of Closure in the Traditional Novel.* Princeton: Princeton UP, 1981

Mitchell, Juliet. *Mad Men and Medusas: Reclaiming Hysteria.* New York: Basic Books, 2000.

Pease, Donald. "National Narratives, Postnational Narration." *Modern Fiction Studies* 43.1 (Spring 1997). 1–23.

Pinero, Arthur Wing. *Trelawny of the 'Wells' and Other Plays.* Oxford: OUP, 1995.

Rabaté, Jean-Michel. *The Future of Theory.* Oxford: Blackwell Publishers, 2002.

———. *Jacques Lacan: Psychoanalysis and the Subject of Literature.* London: Palgrave, 2001.

Ragland, Ellie. *Essays on the Pleasures of Death: From Freud to Lacan.* London and New York: Routledge, 1995.

Rancière, Jacques. "What aesthetics can mean." *From an Aesthetic Point of View: Philosophy, Art and the Senses.* Ed. Peter Osborne. London: Serpent's Tail, 2000. 13–33.

Robinson, Michael. "Acting Women: the performing self and the late nineteenth century." *Comparative Criticism* 14 (1992). 3–24.

Roe, Sue. *Estella: Her Expectations.* Brighton: Harvester, 1982.

Rose, Jacqueline. *Why War?—Psychoanalysis, Politics, and the Return to Melanie Klein.* Oxford: Blackwell, 1993.

Rowell, George, ed. *Nineteenth Century Plays.* Oxford and New York. OUP, 1972.

Rowell, George, *Victorian Dramatic Criticism.* London: Methuen, 1971.

Rushdie, Salman. *Satanic Verses.* Delaware: Consortium Inc., 1992.

Said, Edward. *Beginnings: Intention and Method.* New York: Columbia UP, 1985.

Slater, Michael, and John Drew, eds. *The Dent Uniform Edition of Dickens's Journalism: The Uncommercial Traveller and Other Papers, 1859–1870.* Vol. 4. By Charles Dickens. London: Dent, 2000.

Seigel, Carol. "Postmodern Women Novelists Review Victorian Male Masochism." *Genders* 11 (Fall 1991): 1–16.

Shepherd, Simon, and Peter Womack. *English Drama: A Cultural History.* Oxford: Blackwell Publishers, 1996.

Showalter, Elaine. *The Female Malady: Women, Madness, and English Culture: 1830–1980.* New York: Penguin Books, 1985.

———. *Hystories: Hysterical Epidemics and Modern Culture.* London: Picador, 1997.

———. "Rivers and Sassoon: The Inscription of Male Gender Anxieties." *Behind the Lines: Gender and the Two World Wars.* Ed. Margaret Randolph Higonnet et al. New Haven and London: Yale UP, 1987. 61–69.

Silverman, Kaja. *Male Subjectivity at the Margins.* New York: Routledge, 1992.

Slater, M. *Two Classic Melodramas: Maria Marten and Sweeney Todd.* London: Gerald Howe, 1928.

Spivak, Gayatri Chakravorty. "Theory in the Margin: Coetzee's *Foe* reading Defoe's *Crusoe/Roxana. Consequences of Theory.* Ed. Jonathan Arac and Barbara Johnson. Baltimore: Johns Hopkins UP, 1991. 154–80.

Sprengnether, Madelon. *The Spectral Mother: Freud, Feminism, and Psychoanalysis.* Ithaca: Cornell UP, 1990.

Stallybrass, Peter, and Allon White. *The Poetics and Politics of Transgression.* Ithaca: Cornell UP, 1986.

Taylor, Eugene. Lecture 3 in *William James on Exceptional Mental States: the 1896 Lowell Lectures.* Amherst: U of Massachusetts P, 1984.

Varadharajan, Asha. *Exotic Parodies: Subjectivity in Adorno, Said, and Spivak.* Minneapolis: U of Minnesota P, 1995.

Viera, Else Rebeiro Pires. "Liberating Calibans: Readings of *Antropofagia* and Haroldo de Campos's poetics of transcreation." *Post-colonial Translation: Theory and Practice.* Ed. Susan Basnett and Harish Trivedi. London: Routledge, 1999. 95–113.

Williams, Raymond. *The English Novel from Dickens to Lawrence.* London: Chatto and Windus, 1970.

Woolf, Virginia. *Mrs Dalloway.* New York and London: Harcourt Brace and Co., 1925.

Wright, Elizabeth, ed. *Feminism and Psychoanalysis: A Critical Dictionary.* Oxford: Blackwell, 1992.

Žižek, Slavoj. *The Metastases of Enjoyment.* New York: Verso, 1994.

———. *The Sublime Object of Ideology.* London: Verso, 1989.

———. *Tarrying with the Negative: Kant, Hegel, and the Critique of Ideology.* Durham: Duke UP, 1993.

———. *The Ticklish Subject: The Absent Centre of Political Ontology.* London: Verso, 2000.

———. "The Truth Arises from Misrecognition." *Lacan and the Subject of Language.* Ed. Ellie Ragland-Sullivan and Mark Bracher. New York: Routledge, 1991.

Index